Technological Turf Wars

Technological Turf Wars

A Case Study of the Computer Antivirus Industry

Jessica Johnston

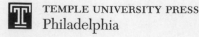

TEMPLE UNIVERSITY PRESS
Philadelphia

Jessica Johnston is a senior lecturer in the American Studies program at the University of Canterbury, New Zealand. She is the author of *The American Body in Context*.

Temple University Press
1601 North Broad Street
Philadelphia PA 19122
www.temple.edu/tempress

⊗The paper used in this publication meets the requirements of the American National Standard for Information Sciences—Permanence of Paper for Printed Library Materials, ANSI Z39.48-1992

Library of Congress Cataloging-in-Publication Data

Johnston, Jessica R., 1952–
    Technological turf wars : a case study of the computer antivirus industry / Jessica Johnston.
        p. cm.
    Includes bibliographical references and index.
    ISBN 978-1-59213-881-4 (cloth : alk. paper)—ISBN 978-1-59213-882-1 (pbk. : alk. paper)   1. Computer security—Case studies.   2. Computer viruses—Prevention—Case studies.   3. Computer industry—Case studies.
I. Title.
    QA76.9.A25J57   2008
    005.8—dc22
                                                                    2008012514

2 4 6 8 9 7 5 3 1

To Betty

Contents

Acknowledgments

I would like to thank all those people who agreed to be interviewed for their time, their considered opinions, and their perspectives. This book would not have been possible without your insights. I would also like to thank Howard McNaughton for his belief in the project. The book was completed during a period of deep cutbacks and restructuring at the University of Canterbury. I would like to express my appreciation to Nick, Cornelia, and Gwen for their support during this difficult time.

Introduction

Computer security is a technical and social problem. It is just as much about social relationships as it is about computers as tools. Internet security professionals are as concerned with how people use information as they are with how machines manipulate and process that information. This book is a case study of how the knowledge systems articulated by computer antivirus industry professionals affect technological security. It analyzes the tensions and political dilemmas at the heart of the interrelationships among science, technology, and society.

All technologies involve 'scripts'. A computer virus is a metaphor that generates images of global viral epidemics and outbreaks, of infectious code reeking havoc on personal computers and global information networks, and of machines that no longer respond to or are under our control. The reality of infected computers generates an entire industry seemingly dedicated to protecting computers and their users from infection, and disinfecting those that succumb. Indeed, those who work within the antivirus industry perpetuate this scripted imagery, and consider themselves part of a security force that polices the 'dark alleys' of the 'information superhighway'.

Based on qualitative interviews over six years with various professionals within the antivirus industry, this book explores changing definitions of security and technological threats to corporate communications within the global marketplace. Grounded in these professionals' own words and attitudes, it highlights the complexity of the issues surrounding the antivirus industry's perspectives of virus writers and spammers, its negotiations with transnational corporations within a techno-capitalist economy, and its interactions with global corporations as end users.

This book also provides a theoretical reflection on the development of technological artifacts. Grounded in the science and technology studies paradigm, it examines how these antivirus professionals' interpretations, economic interests, and disciplinary conflicts affect the production of computer security technology. The competing and cooperating social groups within the industry attempt to achieve industry consensus and technological stabilization, endeavoring to 'black box' or frame certain aspects of antivirus software as transparent, unambiguous, and thus not needing further analysis (Latour 1999). The negotiations, persuasions, and even the disciplinary actions for those who deviate from industry protocols have real-world effects on this technological product. Therefore this book is also about how technology can never be 'black–boxed'. At the beginning of the twenty-first century's culture of fear, antivirus technologies have increasingly become sites of negotiations as industry workers battle over various definitions of threat and disparate interpretations of computer security.

This book examines the history of the antivirus industry and its intersection with the advance of information capitalism. The antivirus industry's foundation is in the mythical beginnings of the open source movement, where computer experts freely distributed their knowledge and worked cooperatively on solving technical problems and threats to the internet, above and outside the pressures of the marketplace. However, antivirus software today is also a consumer product bought and sold in the global marketplace. Industry experts compete in how to best protect information and corporate money in the growth of the high-tech transnational economic system. While industry professionals articulate the empowering processes of openness and collectivity, they also must negotiate their professional lives shaped by their immersion within global capital flows.

Tension arises from the industry professionals' negotiations between generating profit and protecting the internet. They must address the changing 'discourses of danger' in response to transformations of both technologies and escalating world crises. The compromises around these negotiations inform the professionals working within this industry by providing a vocabulary of motives, a sense of identity, values and prevailing concepts of organizational work and worth, and an industry logic. These compromises, however, are addressed differently between the various segments of the industry, and as such are continually contested.

This book is therefore also about the constant shifting between technological objects that appear as neutral—networks, computer code, e-mail programs, and the internet—and the social and ethical values embedded in these objects by the various industry segments. These antivirus industry professionals battle in the global marketplace over malware exploits, transformations of technology, and definitions of 'security'. By documenting these struggles, this book brings alive both the human and the technological and illuminates the seemingly invisible values and ideals networked into the lines of code within antivirus products.

Hackers

I wish to make it clear that this book does not purport to be a depiction of the hacking culture. It is written as a contribution to ongoing analysis of the information age and its institutions of social control and definitions of deviance. Other writers have provided detailed descriptions of the origins and social organization of hackers. This book, while being grateful for such efforts, is written with a different aim. While drawing upon and using their analyses of hackers, this book is about the antivirus industry and its perspective of the world, which includes the industry's stigmatization of, negotiations with, and dependency on these malware writers and the code they write.

The industry's construction of virus writers is not simple or one-sided. Definitions of crime and deviance reflect and influence transformations of social structures. Over the course of the interviews, the antivirus industry's stigmatization of virus writers ranged from juvenile delinquents to 'script-kiddies', to the Russian mafia, and to multimillionaire spammers. These changing definitions arose in relation to geopolitical transformations and advancing technologies, and the interrelated issues of ideological control over those technologies. "[T]he struggle around the definition of crime and deviance is located within the field of action that is constituted by plural and even conflicting efforts at producing control" (Melossi 1994, 205). The effort at securing technological control over the flow of global information is at the heart of the antivirus industry.

There is a growing body of literature about hackers, virus writers, and various aspects of cyber crime. Pekka Himanen (2001) in *The Hacker Ethic: A Radical Approach to the Philosophy of Business* corrects the misperception that 'hackers' are merely teenage misfits glued to their computers. He explains how the background philosophy and positive definition of hackers as 'passionate programmers' originated in the early 1960s. This definition suggests hackers are those people who, regardless of the field in which they work, do what they do for personal satisfaction and the altruism of furthering their area of interest. The other significant element of the hacker ethic that Himanen identifies is the duty to share discoveries and interesting information with like-minded people, and the accompanying peer recognition from that sharing. Hackers enter into this information creation and exchange motivated by enthusiasm, joy, and passion, not just money. Central to the hacker ethic is this task-centric orientation that Himanen contrasts to the time-centric, external reward, and motivation approach of the Protestant work ethic. Generally, the hacker ethic is not motivated by external hierarchies or rules from above, and according to Himanen, it is the 'creative spirit' and driving force of individuals in the information age. Himanen identifies the 'cracker' as the exploitive and malevolent offshoot of the hacker. While Himanen specifies the differences between these two labels, cracker as a deviant label never 'catches on' or reaches cultural iconic status, but instead is almost invisible in popular jargon. Negative computer exploits become attached to the term 'hackers'.

In many ways, Himanen's positive review of the hacker ethic describes the work ethic of antivirus industry professionals. They, too, articulate a task-centric approach to their jobs, and are motivated by the joy, passion, and enthusiasm of problem solving. They are 'on call 24/7', dedicating themselves to solving the latest malware exploit. However, in comparison to Himanen's hacker work ethic, similarities stop there. This enthusiasm and dedication for problem solving articulated by antivirus industry professionals are in support of and funded by large amounts of corporate money. While sharing Himanen's hacker work ethic, antivirus professionals exist to protect corporate information, and to stop, contain, or reverse damage to information caused by the release of malware. This (dis)similarity is at the core of the antivirus industry. The hacker ethic of information sharing, a non-monetary orientation, and a task-centric focus all become points of tension and conflict as these antivirus industry professionals attempt to negotiate the competing logics. This book is an examination of those contestations and their effect on antivirus technological innovation.

The Hacker Manifesto by McKensie Wark (2004) also offers a Marxist framework for understanding the emergence of a 'hacker class'. He also examines institutional forces that are generated to resist it. Wark theorizes that the hacker class is needed by the 'vectorialist class' (informational entrepreneurs) to do their actual work. The inventors, the imaginaries, and the visionaries of technology's potential all belong to Wark's hacker class. They remain free, outside the bounds of financial influences, and cannot be completely controlled. The Hacker Manifesto identifies many of the tensions articulated by antivirus professionals as central to their industry. The mythical beginnings of the internet and many of Wark's critical aphorisms, such as "information wants to be free but is everywhere in chains," are supported by the antivirus professional's own ideological position (Wark 2004, 135).

Indeed, antivirus professionals support many of Wark's assumptions. They suggest that their industry and hackers operate within a similar technological and information-saturated world. Verifying Wark's oppositional structures, antivirus industry professionals suggest that the information society is affected by a strategic dance between the 'white hat' and the 'black hat' technologists. Antivirus professionals, as 'white hats', both work for and within the system. They must negotiate with the state, with transnational corporations, and with the media to protect corporate financial flows. Yet, their professional identities and the logic of the industry are dependent upon the 'black hat' hackers they demonize. The tensions and double-speak that arise out of the similar technological movements within this strategic dance are fascinating.

A researcher who has interviewed and researched the philosophies, ethical positions, and mind-sets of 'black hat' virus writers is Sarah Gordon. Gordon challenged the idea of virus writers as a monolithic group, and has documented the multiple world views of many malware writers. In 1994, she compared various virus writer groupings—adolescents, university students, adults, and ex-virus writers—and evaluated their stated rationales for writing viruses. All except the 'adults' were judged to be normal on the Kohlberg scale of age-related ethical development (Gordon 1994). They wrote viruses for various reasons, but the majority could not be conceptualized as unethical for their developmental level.

Douglas Thomas and Brian Loader (2000) in *Cybercrime: Law Enforcement, Security, and Surveillance in the Information Age* also identify several motives of computer virus writers. Through case studies and critical analysis of hacker discourse, they also highlight the range of malware writers' intention such as experimentation or political activism. In 2000, these authors suggested that most hackers engaged in a cooperative spirit of inquiry and investigation and were more interested in finding, sharing, and discussing software loopholes in order to understand and improve technology, rather than exploiting those loopholes for selfish or unethical purposes.

From the many books and articles published before 2000, hackers and computer virus writers had been seen by many as, if not heroes challenging technological code as a form of social control, then merely misguided delinquents needing education about the real-world consequences of their actions. Acknowledging the research into and with these virus writers, this book documents the antivirus industry's evolution in correspondence with the continual transformation of internet crimes. The further development and evolution of the internet and the Web since 2000 has created a more efficient means for people to gather and sort information and make online purchases 24/7. These same technologies have also ushered in new waves of criminal activity. Interviews for this book began in 2000, when the security industry was targeting 'script-kiddies' and the virus writers who were just experimenting. By 2006, however, the image of these writers changed. Malware writers were organized into high-tech forms of criminal behavior, stealing identities and targeting global systems for profit. Today, their mafia-like organizations around the world have also become global and informational, reflecting the flows of global commerce. While spam was once a mere annoyance, today it is used by organized crime networks with botnets seeding infected machines with adware and hosting fraudulent e-commerce or banking Web sites. These transformations of the 'dark alleys' of the information superhighway both influence and reflect the antivirus industry technology, as it attempts "plural and conflicting efforts at producing control" (Melossi 1994).

Theoretical Groundings

The term 'computer virus' is a metaphor that combines the biological imagery of viral epidemics and outbreaks with high-tech global informatics. Many authors have commented upon this coupling. Deborah Lupton suggested in 1994 that the metaphor of a computer virus reveals our ambivalent attitude toward new technologies. She suggested that computer viruses refer to the "computer technology's parasitical potential to invade and take control from within" (Lupton 1994, 566). Stefan Helmreich (2000) drew on David Harvey (1990) and Emily Martin (1994) to characterize computer viruses as "employing language reminiscent of that used to describe 'bodies' of nation-states under military threat from without and within" (Helmreich 2000, 473). In 2005, Jussi Parikka, citing Humberto Maturana, stated, "During the past few decades, biological creatures like viruses, worms, bugs, and bacteria seem to have migrated from the natural habitats to ecologies of silicone [sic] and electricity" (Parikka 2005, 1). The hybridity at the core of the computer virus metaphor serves as a ripe field for academic analysis.

This book, however, complicates this theoretical orientation. It focuses on those whose daily enterprise seeks to, if not destroy, at least contain the effects of this coupling. The antivirus industry works within and against the narratives of a body/machine metaphor as industry workers research, develop, and use antivirus products. At its most basic, the antivirus product is computer code designed to contain other strings of self-replicating computer code. The antivirus product then is the culmination of scientific research, industry negotiations, and the application of marketing in an economy based on both the fear of invasions and faith in technological progress. As such, it is a prime object for science and technology studies.

Researchers in the field of science and technology studies have produced a great deal of scholarship that documents and analyzes the social shaping of technology (MacKenzie and Wajcman 1985; Bijker

1995). An important area of this scholarship is the Social Construction of Technology (SCOT), which explores the various human processes that affect the discovery, design, development, and use of technological artifacts. This field of research challenges the idea of technological determinism, which neutralizes or renders invisible the material conditions of development and technological practices, and the social environments within and through which technologies originate and operate. These researchers do not conceptualize IT artifacts as stable, discrete, independent, or fixed (Orlikowski and Lacono 2001).

Instead, researchers in this field focus on how technological design is an open process that can produce different outcomes depending on the social circumstances of development. Using rich case studies of technological invention and development, social constructivist research examines how interpretations, social interests, and disciplinary conflicts shape the production of a technology by framing its cultural meanings and the social interactions among relevant social groups (Orlikowski and Lacono 2001). No one person or group creates a technological artifact. Negotiations and various knowledges, observations, and goals allow for multiple paths toward that development. Technological artifacts are in this sense 'under determined' and are the product of flexible interpretations and power relationships.

These contestations and negotiations between social groups and their effects on the technological artifact are relevant areas of study in the antivirus industry. Various social groups, with different rankings and statuses, and with different invested positions and interpretations labor to see their vision of antivirus software realized. The cultural contexts of those groups, their taken-for-granted assumptions, and their social situation within the larger sociocultural environment all come to affect the technological artifact. Who is included and who is excluded, who has what access to what information, what barriers are crossed or raised and by whom, what compromises are brokered, what is left silenced and unspoken, or not even conceptualized because of variations in such factors as gender, race, or class backgrounds—all these variables come to affect the technological artifact. For the antivirus industry, power, contestation, inequality, and hierarchy inscribe the industry and shape the production of antivirus software. This book reveals how these intervening mechanisms, having little to do with the antivirus technology per se, (re)shape the software product.

Another key point of SCOT analysis is that artifact development is 'finished' only when the various groups reach a consensus. "Design ceases not because the artifact works in some objective sense but because the set of relevant social groups accepts that it works for them" (Bijker 1995, 270). This acceptance leads to a sense of 'closure' and 'stabilization' with no further implementation or further design modifications. If there are any lingering problems, they are redefined as insignificant.

However, recent scholarship questions the definitions and perceptions of 'closure' and technological 'stabilization'. IT artifacts are not static and unchanging. They are dynamic because "new materials are invented, different features are developed, existing functions fail and are corrected, new standards are set, and users adapt the artifact for new and different uses" (Orlikowski and Barley 2001). Technological artifacts in this sense are never stable or closed. Within the antivirus industry, the antivirus product is constantly being modified and adapted to changing technological transformations and to evolving corporate needs. Corporate end users engage in the co-construction of their technologies as vendors form end user focus groups to help inform their researchers, as product-developers reach out to consumers to understand their preferences, and as corporate end users retool their antivirus products to fit their corporate needs. Science and Technology Studies researchers increasingly identify this type of ambiguity between producers' open-ended artifacts and users' sanctioned and unsanctioned modifications as important areas of current research.

Technological artifacts are, in this sense, open and evolving. They are also granted power. Similar to the microbes in Bruno Latour's (1988) analysis of the "Pasteurization of France," computer code can destroy or protect. Latour's actor–network theory (ANT) suggests that the human and the nonhuman are entwined and inseparable, a concept of interconnectedness that is usually overlooked in both academic analysis and our daily interactions. Drawing on actor–network theory, computer code is rearticulated as actively intervening, both positively and negatively, in our economy, in our faith in technology, and in our relationships. Antivirus experts are authorized and empowered by the behavior of computer code. Indeed, the antivirus industry conceptualizes itself as the necessary gatekeepers watching and protecting the global economy against the actions of computer code. The actions of computer code are important as antivirus industry professionals respond to outbreaks and dedicate their professional lives to eradicating the effects of malware. Latour's ANT helps bring this interaction between industry professionals and the actions of the computer code into the foreground.

The other foundational theorist for this book is Michel Foucault. Much of the exploration of the power relationships within the antivirus industry draws upon Foucualt's (1972) analysis of the power/knowledge nexus. Foucault sees power as strategies and influences running through networks; these strategies and influences are seemingly invisible and taken for granted as 'natural' and inevitable. One of the central concerns of Foucault's work is to dispel these seeming self-evidences. His work illuminates how even familiar and taken-for-granted assumptions of authority and common sense are not 'natural' or part of a naturally existing order. Through a number of different examples from hospitals to prisons, Foucault has shown how what counts as truth and knowledge depends on, or is determined by, the conceptual system in operation (Casey 1995).

Within the antivirus industry, there are two conflicting conceptual systems in operation. One is a technical hierarchy, based on a faith in the technological knowledge and research proficiency of the antivirus expert. Reflecting cyberspace generally, at the top of the cultural construct that led to the creation of the internet is the techno-meritocratic culture of scientific and technological excellence, emerging essentially from big science and the academic world (Castells 2001). This conceptual system is based on sharing research, open discussions, and academic debates, and is even foundational to the positive elements of the hacker work ethic discussed earlier. Both the hackers' and the antivirus industry's status as technological experts and their recognition through their community of peers, is enmeshed within and is a part of this culture of techno-meritocracy. However, the antivirus industry is a for-profit endeavor. And the conceptual orientation of the corporate business system is closed and competitive, where research results are guarded secrets. Corporate research and development, the results from R&D, are valuable, profitable, and protected as such. Within the antivirus industry, research and development merges with bottom-line profits and industry rankings. This conflict between cooperative and competitive systems, between scientific and corporate research ideals, generates various definitions of, knowledge about, and expertise in computer code, security threats, and end users' needs.

Information Capitalism

The internet evolved from merely a complex communication system into a major new arena for capital accumulation and the operations of global capital (Sassen 2002; Castells 1996). The power relations of the older manufacturing capitalism have been reconfigured on a global scale around information-driven systems. This brand of information capitalism is profoundly different from its historical predecessors. According to Manuel Castells (1996), information capitalism has three fundamentally distinctive features: it is global and instantaneous; it is structured to a large extent around a network of information flows; and capital is realized, invested, and accumulated mainly in these spheres of circulation. Access to these networks of information flows then becomes vitally important. Indeed, Castells suggests that ownership and property relations have been replaced in the information age by the ability to access information and generate intellectual capital. Access to technological know-how is at the root of productivity and competitiveness. Consequently, new patterns of inequality emerge on the basis of reduced access to information. New concentrations of 'information wealth', global elites, and the 'informational bourgeoisie' dominate the arenas of this information society.

Access and intellectual capital are key concepts for understanding the antivirus industry. As the gatekeepers of information flows, as the digital fingers on the pulse/flow of information, as the security point/node in the flow of information on the internet, industry professionals monitor these flows for threats. Through their products, they assure the continued 'frictionless' circulation of these flows. Based on their knowledge and technical expertise, these industry professionals turn their information into capital as they transform their knowledge and computer code into products that protect threatened circulation flows. Because of this position in the information age, they profit financially, both as individuals and as businesses, as long as the threats persist.

While working to secure the information society, eruptions occur inside the industry as different segments of the industry also vie for the power to control the security surrounding information capital. Through erecting knowledge monopolies and disciplinary exclusions, their various knowledges become a powerful form of intellectual property. These various industry segments simultaneously produce, reproduce, and are victimized by the ability to channel the circulation of information flows. This book is a structural and systemic analysis of how antivirus technologies are embedded in these complex interdependent networks, and how they are shaped by these broader social, economic, and political institutional influences.

Method

I am an outsider to the antivirus industry. My background is in anthropology and culture studies with a theoretical interest in the social conditions structuring technology. Having attended several of the Virus Bulletin International Conferences, going to the sessions and listening to questions after the sessions, as well as the conversations over breakfasts, lunches, dinners, . . . and drinks, I began sensing a subtly shifting power dynamic within, what I had thought to be, a relatively stable set of associations. As industry professionals attempted to respond to the changes in technology, in personnel, and in the definitions of threats and security, I began to see symbolic and some not so symbolic challenges to previously revered authorities and industry groups. Antivirus professionals were re-defining themselves and their industry within what they portrayed as an increasingly technocratic and insecure global economy. This book is one perspective of these changing social relations as the antivirus industry negotiated issues of security and profit in an increasingly technologically vulnerable world.

Of the multiple divergent perspectives that began to emerge in the conferences' end-of-session questions and in personal conversations with both presenters and attendees, the most obvious and seemingly most misunderstood issues were grounded in the conflicting interests, attitudes, and perspectives held between antivirus developers and IT administrators as the developers' corporate customers. The diversity was articulated in their contradictory goals, directions, and the services generally expected of and provided by the industry. However, in listening to these divergent worldviews being expressed by variously-situated individuals, I realized that each took for granted that their perspective was universally understood and absorbed. Each assumed the other was and should be operating within the same reference points.

In order to investigate this seeming discrepancy, I scheduled interviews with several IT administrators of the biggest corporate representatives at these conferences and many of the product managers of the largest antivirus developers. I conducted many of these interviews at the Virus Bulletin International Conference in Orlando, Florida, and at the Association of Antivirus Asian Researchers Conference in Tokyo, Japan—both in 2000. I also interviewed IT administrators of large corporations outside the Virus Bulletin conference world, specifically targeting those who had never attended an antivirus conference. I conducted follow-up interviews over the next six years as personnel changed, as new threats emerged, and as the industry adapted.

Originally I had not conceptualized antivirus researchers as related to the divergent perspectives between IT administrators and antivirus product managers. I saw antivirus researchers as an economically integrated, intimate part of the developers' market orientation, and consequently not central to my sense of the conflicting points of view articulated between corporate customers and the antivirus product developers. But the more I talked with the product developers, the more they recommended I needed to include the antivirus researchers as men who have the power to guide and influence both the direction and the products of the entire industry.[1] I listened to these managers as 'native' experts and expanded the parameters of my research to include the technological researchers and their perspective of their industry. Consequently, I have interviewed thirty-three individuals within the antivirus industry distributed across corporate IT administrators in charge of computer security, antivirus product managers and vendors, and antivirus researchers.

The three categories of workers within the antivirus industry, the corporate IT managers, the vendors, and the researchers, do not exist independently of each other. In fact it was often the moments when

---

[1] While 'men' is used here, six women within the various levels of the antivirus industry granted me the privilege of interviewing them and allowed me to record their insights into their world. Gender is a significant factor that needs to be addressed within the antivirus industry and is discussed in the final chapter, "Situated Exclusions and Reinforced Power." To protect the women's anonymity, all respondents are identified as male.

the boundaries between these categories blurred, such as when a virus outbreak occurred, that led to questions about who had the appropriate knowledge and information to protect the internet. Was it the frontline IT manager who first gathered the information about the virus attacking his network? Or was it the vendor who had multiple IT managers' reports of the virus attacking the network? Or was it the researcher who analyzed the computer code in order to provide a solution? Discussion about these socially-situated knowledge sites highlighted the tensions of the knowledge/power nexus. It was this blurring or leakage between competing definitions and categories that enabled dominant, commonsense notions of security to become problematic as these workers discussed their perspectives, their roles, and their sense of their socially-situated exclusive knowledges.

Throughout the six years of interviewing, changes in broader social and cultural structures affected the industry. Security issues exploded around 9/11 and the U.S. government's war on terror, Microsoft changed from being the target of virus writers' exploits to a supplier of antivirus products for the home market, and several new technologies came to market while others became outdated. Individually, some of the original participants changed jobs, some quit the industry, and new recruits joined the industry. Indeed, each participant's engagements with the industry is experienced differently and has changed and shifted in multiple and various ways over the years.

There is a need to highlight the partiality and constructed nature of any research project because of all these changes and transformations, and these multiple voices and shifting subject positions (Lather 2004; Fine 1994). The antivirus industry was and continues to be adapting and transforming. The voices and analysis gathered here are limited by the specific people who agreed to be interviewed, the historical changes, and the erratic features of a globalized high-tech economy. The conclusions then are also partial and based on the perspectives given at the time, and over time, from a self-selected group of people in an industry coping with turn-of-the-century fractures, ruptures, and continuities.

My interviews and analysis are based on a post-positivist theoretical orientation that questions the universality of facts and truths. In broad contrast to the neutral, objectivist stance of the positivist, a post-positivist employing qualitative research methods asserts her subjectivity and the partialness of her research (Lather 2004; Fine 1994). All research settings are permeated with inequalities and power relations that ultimately resolve themselves in favor of the researcher (Bloom 1996). I acknowledge the ways that both researcher and researched actively construct the stories and interpretations on which this final research text is based. However, I also accept responsibility for the production of the final text and my authoritative claim to knowledge about this industry (Harrison, MacGibbon, and Morton 2001).

All informants' names have been changed and identifying characteristics have been eliminated. All interviews were taped with the permission of the respondents and were transcribed. The interview questions were loosely structured to cover the interviewees' backgrounds and experiences in the antivirus industry, a description of their jobs, its challenges and rewards, and their definitions and attitudes toward other job categories within the industry. Questions also focused on the variously occurring current world and industry events and corresponding (re)definitions of threat and security that accompanied them.

All interviews were analyzed applying the principles of grounded theory such as familiarization, data exploration, reflection and data sense making, and linking of emerging patterns (Easterby-Smith, Thorpe, and Lowe 1991). Using the above typology, the processes, the common as well as differing practices, and espoused industry values were identified.

The stories I have chosen to use to illustrate my analysis represent some moments in an evolving engagement with individuals negotiating changes in their working lives on the high-tech edge of a continually transforming information economy. Their ongoing negotiations are always contextual and contingent, and a major aim of this book is to explore some of that complexity in relation to computer security at the turn of the twenty-first century. Of course the researcher has the ultimate control and authority over the text she produces; it is her interpretations, her choices of material, and her representations of others' stories that prevail in any written work she produces. What follows, then, is my representation of the research stories I collected during the six years of contact with the antivirus industry.

I Naming the Threat

The problem is that once you release a virus it has a life of its own. It starts spreading and you have virtually no control over it.

(DANIEL — ANTIVIRUS RESEARCHER)

Naming the Computer Virus Threat

On November 4, 1988, computers around the Advanced Research Projects Agency Network (ARPANET), the forerunner to today's internet, suddenly and dramatically slowed down. They were sluggish, some eventually becoming completely unresponsive. Unnecessary and unneeded data had interfered with their operations. And these clogging processes swiftly disseminated around the globe. In *Technopoly*, Neil Postman identifies how the popularization of the computer virus metaphor began:

> The early hypothesis was that a software program had attached itself to other programs, a situation which is called (in another human–machine metaphor) a 'virus'. As it happened, the intruder was a self-contained program explicitly designed to disable computers, which is called a 'worm'. But the technically incorrect term 'virus' stuck, no doubt because of its familiarity and its human connections. . . . [N]ewspapers noted that the computers were 'infected', that the virus was 'virulent' and 'contagious', that attempts were made to 'quarantine' the infected

computers, that attempts were also being made to 'sterilize' the network.

(Postman 1993, 113)

The explanation of the computer code that disrupted global information flows was structured through metaphors of highly infectious diseases with corresponding references to outbreaks and contagion. Alan Solomon, the name behind Dr. Solomon's Anti-Virus Toolkit, a veteran antivirus researcher with a Ph.D. in economics, critiqued the virus metaphor, suggesting that this medical/biological metaphor of 'virus' is 'too emotive' (Jordan and Taylor 1998). Instead, he proposed 'weeds' as a more appropriate concept for describing the spread of computer code. Indeed, this kind of plant metaphor could have been developed though seeds, spores, pollen, and weed-resistant analogies. The plant/weed metaphor could also expand the current use of 'worm' with attacks of maggots, larvae, and termites with corresponding references to antivirus (AV) professionals located within an anti-weed industry as gardeners, farmers, or exterminators, and their products as 'weed whackers' or 'herbicides'.

This weed metaphor never gained the currency of the virus metaphor in a high-tech world dealing with acquired immune deficiency syndrome (AIDS). Currently, the media, government, and security professionals use the virus metaphor to focus attention on the 'health' of our computers and our networks. Infections by computer viruses today highlight the speed and importance surrounding significant disruptions to the global flow of information in a fast-paced, interconnected yet vulnerable technological society.

Embodiment Metaphors

Definition of Metaphor

The dominance of the virus over the weed metaphor highlights how metaphors are not used merely as decorative speech or convenient economies of expression (Johnson 1987; Lakeoff and Johnson 1980). The applicability or relevance of a metaphor depends on the interactive processes of an entire communication system, with seemingly separate categories interacting with the implications from others. This interactive process entails reflections and projections—structures from one domain influence and order the understanding of others, generating a reciprocal new understanding that 'rings true' within the cultural knowledge system. This interlinked new image is more than just the combination of separate images; it suggests larger and more integrated connections between them.

The meaning of a metaphor then is not simply a list of properties and relations shared by concepts. An emergent structured meaning complex is created, one that cannot be broken into individualistic parts without destroying the crucial relations between them. The key issue in analyzing a metaphor is to determine which features are metaphorically transferred and which are left behind, and of course the significance of those inclusions and exclusions. In this sense, the computer virus metaphor is not reducible to the two images of a virus and a computer, but entails a stretching and reorganizing of the conceptual boundaries inherent within both.

Popular culture has explored some of the complexities and tensions surrounding the computer virus metaphor, from movies such as *Sneakers* (1992) and *Terminator 3* (2003), to television shows such as *Star Trek: The Next Generation* "Contagion," *Stargate SG1* "The Entity," *Stargate Atlantis* "The Intruder," and *Battlestar Galactica,* "Flight of the Phoenix." In many of these popular culture texts, representations of the body/machine interface display fears about the penetration of technology—that humans become appendages of it rather than its master; that they cannot resist it; that technology negatively changes their lives forever; that they serve technology, rather than the reverse; that technologies are fast outstripping human abilities. Those fears are also attributed to the technology itself—as a source of power, as potentially destructive, as changing fundamentally the understanding of 'human'.

This anxiety toward technology operates within a wider, general social climate of unease that is fueled by the contemporary prominence of a number of biological infections: AIDS, Ebola, severe acute respiratory syndrome (SARS), and avian flu. The biological virus is seen as a parasitic organism, invading and damaging the body's cells while using those cells to replicate its own form. Similarly, the computer virus is self-replicating code capable of transforming files or other programs on a computer and spreading itself throughout the network. One vendor discussed a presentation he gave to prospective customers about computer virus outbreaks:

VENDOR GARY: I have a presentation that I've been giving
lately and I now have this one slide that comes up but it
just has the word 'outbreak', with an exclamation point at
the end. And I say this has now become the least favorite
word in my vocabulary. And I never even used it before
because I didn't do any biology when I was in school, and
so I didn't know anything about, you know, AIDS outbreak, or Ebola outbreak, or whatever the case may be.
But now it's a very bad word.

The identification of information technology (IT)-based super-
viruses exists within this climate of catastrophic pandemics, each biological and technological infection affecting the metaphoric
networks at play within the culture, generating a culturally receptive
environment for each. These threatening embodied experiences
bubble up into language, reinforcing feedback loops for each. The
hybridity of the 'computer virus' that ensues from these contaminated forms occasions a new relationship between both the body and
technology.

Embodied Metaphors of Contagion

The institutionalization of the medicalization of computer viruses
frames the value of the work of the antivirus professional (Bourdieu
1985, 733). That value defines and is reflected in the markets and marketing of antiviruses—from products entitled "InoculateIT" or variously
incorporating the words 'doctor', 'Dr', and 'vaccine' into their names, to
software packaging with images of hypodermic needles and people
dressed in white lab coats with stethoscopes draped around their necks.
Antivirus professionals confirm and promote this medical life and death
linguistic urgency and the image of the antivirus product as a high-tech
protective health-care service. They also gain legitimacy from articulating themes attached to these virtual life and death struggles.

Computer viruses thus give form to the antivirus community's
sense of identity and distinctiveness. Two corporate end users, one an
IT manager attached to a large city council IT department and another
an IT manager at a large university, highlight this sense of disease and
contamination. Their discussions import medical discourse and popu-

lar anxieties about sexual contamination, and proffer 'safe sex' tips for computer use. The first excerpt illustrates how he discusses the importance of computer viruses with his staff:

> CORPORATE END USER DONALD: Well, I tell them it is always good to practice safe sex, but basically you know, you kind of [laughs]. If you can explain how a virus works in the human body, then you can give rough analogies as to how it works in the computer. And in much of the same types of care that you need to take if you're single on the dating scene sort of thing, where to prevent from, you know, physical contagion, also applies in terms of protecting yourself from an unwanted influence on the computer.

A university IT manager comments about floppy disc infections:

> CORPORATE END USER ANTHONY: Well, computer viruses are like more biological viruses. If people sleep around you're going to get a virus, and the computer's the same. If you're passing discs around you're going to be vulnerable, and of course you don't know where the other person has had their disc [laughs].

Over the six years of interviews, antivirus professionals continually identified the threat of contagion by drawing a direct parallel between the human body and the computer. The simulation of networked disease is prefaced on this understanding of embodied contagion. Individuals/systems begin as pure self-contained entities, but external 'unwanted influences' can corrupt a previously 'pure' and uncontaminated system. In these specific quotes, the acceptance of personal responsibility for safe sex is presented as necessary against 'unprotected contact' with corrupted other body/computer parts. The need for individual unerring defensive measures is highlighted by the body's/computer's ongoing and continual vulnerability. Being socially open to unprotected networked contact is dangerous.

These IT managers use the body to generate discipline through metaphors of contagion and disease, with the threat to the physical body as the point of reference for controlling end users. This safe sex metaphor provides normative interpretations of appropriate situations and actions for both sexual and technological behavior.

The disciplinary power of the safe sex metaphor is also affirmed. The IT managers identify the user's position as corruptible, describing both the individualized and net effects of these infectious interrelationships. Actions are monitored and traceable to specific bodies/computers within the potentially all-seeing circuitry. The safe sex metaphor potentially generates compliance as individuals are told to actively police their own actions both when connecting sexually and when networking with other computers. This message has even been reinforced by vendors handing out self-branded condoms at computer security conferences!

This duality of the networked vulnerable body/computer metaphor challenges much of postmodern theory on technology and the body that 'leaves the meat behind' (Sobchack 1998). Postmodernists theorize that technology is 'dehumanizing' us. They suggest the increasing passivity of the human subject, including a loss of agency and the erasure of the body and identity (Poster 2001; Baudrillard 1975; Haraway 1999). Postmodern theories of the body suggest a loss of corporeal experience within technological communication, which is intimately tied to the implicit loss of an active subject position.

Instead, these quotes demonstrate how the computer virus metaphor draws on images of bodies as active, reactive, and infectious interfaces with the world. These professionals ground and explain technological interactions through phenomenological embodied experiences. They identify how each individual's body/computer is vulnerable and stress the individualized responsibility to be actively aware and cautious about what they allow to be 'inserted' into their personal systems. Individuals must prevent potentially dangerous infections, infections that ultimately affect the rest of the interconnected global population. Both the individual's body and computer are susceptible through interactive communications and must be proactive in response.

Rather than suggesting the body is denied by technology, or that corporeality and identity is lost, the safe sex metaphor illuminates the relationship between the virtual and the real, the informational and the biological, promoting a transformation in the experience and understanding of both the body and the computer. Bodies are re-envisioned as part of a networked circuit of communications, while the computer is represented as vulnerable through its sexualization. Bodily experience in this sense is not denied or transcended, but utilized as a way to explain how interfaces to the network are threatened and must be protected. The corporeal experience of a sexual relationship with another person is not eliminated, but is reconceptualized as establishing an intimate and active connection with many unknown, interacting, and networked others. In this sense, the IT managers encourage individuals to be aware, not only of themselves as embodied, but to take precautions in the act of transmitting bodily fluids/information with other potentially infectious embodied beings/computers.

This corporeal/mechanistic connection narrativizes both the communication process and the technology. It provides a script that draws upon the specific safe sex metaphor while highlighting the embodied dangers and similarities between exchanging computer communications and bodily fluids. It also elides culturally determined identities such as the body's gender, class, disabilities, and ethnicities. These cultural markers evaporate in an all-encompassing universal embodiment that dismisses qualities tying specific individual bodies to their cultural contexts. Within the antivirus industry and their labor against computer viral infections, the body that is always already there is devoid of contemporary cultural specificities. While using the body as an important part of the context for understanding and properly utilizing computer technology, IT managers erase the specific contexts provided by embodiment. This universal body is unmarked by gender, ethnicity, physical disability, or culture.

Networked Viruses

The use of the safe sex metaphor at the network level reveals individuals as one among many others—all connected, 'jacked into' multiple systems, all points *within* a circuit, a circuit that is always open to the world, 24/7, and of course always potentially infecting and contaminating multiple others. It is within this networked communication with others that the spatial frames collapse between each individual body. A corporate IT manager discusses infection by his foreign customers:

> CORPORATE END USER DONALD: They come over here, they plug it in the network, or they share their document, or they place it up on the internal network, and then bang!

Everybody's got it. And it doesn't take long and of course you get not just one virus but multiple viruses. . . .

The effect of individual contagion within the circuit is on the entire integrated networked global system.

RESEARCHER THOMAS: There are so many different people, but it only takes one in the multi-thousand employee corporation to launch an epidemic.

Virus outbreaks are represented as multiplying instantaneously, generating an epidemic. Initially, the individualized body/computer descends from its original state of cleanliness and purity, corrupted through interaction with unprotected others. An epidemic ensues where every networked social relation becomes, in itself, corrupted and corrupting. For the antivirus industry, the networked society is framed through the continual threat of embodied viral epidemics.

This frame of unrelenting potential viral epidemics supplies the grounding for the grand narrative of the antivirus industry. The industry is to supply technical knowledge and innovative software applications in order to develop immune systems and antidotes for infected machines:

VENDOR MARK: I think that this model which we have of producing the antidotes to the viruses when they appear, has followed quite well the speed of some viruses, and with rare exceptions, it has kept up. So with the immune systems, the artificial immune system which we are operating, antivirus software around the globe is protecting and being updated as soon as any threats appear.

The antivirus industry's grand narrative is that it is successfully producing antidotes that update computer software against global viral threats. The 'model' is reactive, responding to virus outbreaks as they appear.

The computer virus metaphor is not then merely a picturesque anthropomorphism. It is grounded in and reflects the profound perception about the relationship of computers and humans and the widespread cultural concerns over the increasing levels of interaction with rapidly changing and evolving information technologies. Epidemics and the development of immune systems are re-visioned as part of a circuit of communication that does not deny bodily experience, but conceives of the body as an interface that continually needs protection. The computer virus is an image that both identifies and collapses the boundaries between the natural and the mechanical. It highlights the concerns about humans and their technologies, their openings and their dependencies, their vulnerabilities and possibilities.

Defining Risk/Threat

At the most basic level, humans construct computer viruses. Computer viruses are merely assembled lines of computer code, not an organic, natural, or biological phenomenon. They are designed to transform computers.

However, defining these assembled lines of computer code as a 'threat' entails identifying what values are threatened, the extent of the threat to those values, and the costs of violating those values. In this sense, 'threat' is a discourse, value-laden and political, reflecting cultural concepts about what needs protection (Krause and Williams 1997; Huysmans 2002). As revealed in the safe sex and epidemic metaphors above, threats also attribute blame by asserting positions of right and wrong, and legitimate formal and informal disciplinary regimes. Thus, computer viruses as technological threat-talk can be viewed as pointing to the fears and ethos of the information society as well as the distribution and sources of power within that society.

In the following quotes, the object of threat is significant. Note what these three differently socially-situated industry professionals identify as threatened and in need of protection:

I: How do you define 'threat'?

VENDOR JASON: It's a case of having enough information to assess the level of risk and then deciding whether or not the cost of protection is greater than or less than the cost of recovery from the damaging effects should that risk realize itself.

RESEARCHER KEITH: What is threat? There is a business threat, because what I do are primarily businesses and so their concern is that there may be some loss to their business as a result of some type of computer-related crime, someone breaking into their network systems and stealing information that causes them a loss, or destroying information which causes them immediate loss.

CORPORATE END USER CHRIS: Well you look at a threat as something that's already—that's achievable, right? The threat is out there. The risk is, your risk assessment, how badly is that threat going to affect your bottom line, how bad is it going to affect business continuity, that's what a risk is.

The topic of threat is identified, then conflated and channeled into financial risk assessments. These three industry professionals focus on the threat to business networks, to the bottom line, and abstract that threat into a risk assessment. Threat is calibrated to express the potential harm of an imagined crisis. It is the best estimate of the probability of a computer-related transgression occurring, and the harm that would result to business continuity should it occur. This risk is then analyzed as a monetary calculation affecting the corporate bottom line. The cost of protection is balanced against the cost of recovery, the damaging effect of information loss is compared to the price of guarding those losses. These quotes highlight the important economic aspects inherent within the antivirus industry's danger discourses. As these quotes suggest, definitions of threats are assessed within the industry as protecting corporate assets and money.

According to Ulrich Beck, modern risks are difficult to calculate because of their scale and magnitude (Beck 1999, 215). No single institution can prevent large-scale risks or compensate for their effects. The prevailing sensibility within a culture based on this risk logic is that of 'the least worst', where concern is not focused on obtaining something 'good', but rather with preventing the worst. Within the antivirus industry, this risk logic and focus on the prevention of the worst is institutionalized and expressed, for example, through the safe sex 'tips' promoted by the IT managers. The safe sex metaphor is part of a normative counterplan, aimed at, but not limited to, applying risk/threat management techniques. The IT managers use the techniques that focus on educating and informing individuals of their responsibilities and their contributions to outbreaks and epidemics. The risk logic/normative counterplan provides scripts for the prevention of infection. These scripted plans are a discourse that represents and contrasts the identities of the irresponsible or victimized body/machine with the informed rescuer/IT manager. It is in this sense both disciplinary and moralistic.

Threats and Virus Writers

The malicious code writer is perceived as the disrupting origin of the threat. In many ways, the virus writer becomes the repository for fears not simply about risks/threats, but also about the breakdown of social order and the ability of the entire legal system to cope with boundaries and divisions in a time of tremendous change. The effort to ground and contextualize these high-tech behaviors is accomplished by connecting them to the stigma of a 'thief'.

> RESEARCHER CHARLES: They are thieves. They are both thieves in the sense of stealing bandwidth and resources. They do harm to equipment in terms of compromising them and making them insecure. And they cause damage to the community both in terms of destroying the value of e-mail and sending out material that is completely inappropriate. How can one respect anything like that?

The descriptive label of 'electronic vandal', or 'cyber thief', is used by many in the industry and is focused on the destruction of the 'value' of electronic communications. The community and commerce of the internet, dependent upon electronic information flows, is made insecure and threatened. People are unable to trust contents of e-mails or Web sites.

Interestingly, while this damage is portrayed as critically affecting the very foundations and values of electronic communications, the cyber thief is negated as nothing more than a petty criminal. In comparison to the professionals within the antivirus industry, virus writers are not seen as technically proficient. Their code is seen as badly written and of poor quality. The majority of 'successful' viruses, according to these professionals, are merely 'lucky' in that they are released within a set of conditions that cause damage the writer generally did not foresee or intend. In this sense, the virus writer, whether a 'script-kiddie' or part of organized crime, is doubly deficient. The virus writer is without morals, and is devoid of intellectual and technical sophistication.

Indeed, many industry professionals reaffirm their superiority in their discussions of a worst-case scenario. Virus writers are conceptualized as technically inadequate, even in their malicious intent.

> CORPORATE END USER EDWARD: I personally think that virus writers could be a lot more malicious than what they are. That's my personal feeling. If it was me, I'd just write something that was, that just would erase something every twelve or thirteen days. It would erase a random file. How long would it take you to realize that was happening, you know? That's the key to it right there. If you just want to be a bastard, that's how I would do something.

> RESEARCHER KEITH: It would be relatively trivial to social engineer a piece of malicious code to, for example, the secretary of the CEO in a big company. You just have a little program sit there and encrypt all the files on her machine and send them to several anonymous e-mail boxes, like throw-away addresses at Hotmail. The person who cleared them, depending on the software you use and which service you use, the person who cleared them could clear them via re-directors so that Hotmail wouldn't be able to go to the FBI or anyone else who tried to investigate with any particularly useful data that would help them track it down. It could be done without the people even knowing it had been done to them. There would be spreadsheets with financial results, projections, blah, blah. There might be customer list information. There could be all kinds of very sensitive information that that person has access to.

These antivirus professionals project a scenario that exploits the secrecy of information. Toying with the idea of private property, their technical expertise allows them to conceptualize erasing and appropriating others' sensitive files. At their will, they can control access and information flow, flex their technological domination and mastery. Other worst-case scenarios mentioned several times included targeting an antivirus vendor. The vendor would then inadvertently spread the outbreak in their updates to their customers, such as large international banks and military sites, that would then infect their employees and customers.

The worst-case scenarios cited above highlight how the antivirus industry shares and even reproduces some of the same technological interests and characteristics of their virus writer counterparts. They too have thought of and could deploy computer code to affect the flow of network communication. The demarcation between 'us' and 'them' divides the world into oppositional categories of 'good' and 'bad'—the social and moral boundaries and divisions structuring the technical world. In this sense there is no such thing as a 'good virus'. Creating a self-replicating program to fix or contain a malicious outbreak is unacceptable, no matter the intention of the virus writer.

> RESEARCHER DANIEL: There is no such thing as a good virus. The mere fact that something is able to self-replicate means that it can land on a system where it can cause damage, just because the author of the thing has not foreseen something, for instance, or because that system didn't exist at the time when the thing was made. The problem is that once you release a virus it has a life of its own, it starts spreading. You have virtually no control over it. So there is no good virus. There is really no need whatsoever to use self-replicating code. Any task that you can do with self-replicating code you can do just as well with non-self-replicating code.

Within the antivirus industry, there is a strict moral underpinning that infuses the creation and use of technological products. Conflating morality and technology, there are only 'bad' viruses and 'bad guys' who create and use them, based not only on their intent, but also on the long-term systemic effects on information systems.

The denigrations of virus writers and the accompanying worst-case scenarios highlight two interconnected points. First, morality and technology are interlinked, and together they structure the identity of the antivirus professional within the industry. The virus writer as the industry doppelganger is dismissed and belittled based on both a lack of morality, and a questionable ability to directly affect economic and technical structures. The antivirus professional could more effectively corrupt the information systems with greater stealth, malicious intent, and success, if so inclined. Through applying the stigma of 'electronic vandal' and 'cyber thief' to the virus writer, the antivirus professional's combined morality and technical expertise is elevated.

Second, within this dichotomized ranking, there still is a recognition of the virus writer's effect on the information society. Even though virus writers lack technical skill, they nevertheless compromise equipment, open files that are protected, and master the deceit inherent in social engineering. They have the ability to effect operations within the programmed hierarchies of the information society, unsettling business routines, challenging firewall-protected servers, and confusing end users. Indeed, the antivirus professional's identity is based on a presumed ability to counter these negative effects on networked communication. Antivirus experts' countermeasures work to assert their professional identities and elevate the morality and expertise of their industry, while also simultaneously denigrating and stigmatizing the virus writer.

The virus writer is then a 'bad guy'. In the fast-paced high-tech world of the information society, the characteristics of these bad guys have changed over time, their demographics, goals, and objects of attack reflect technological transformations. Antivirus industry professionals are aware of how the computer technologies that provide the opportunities for the profitable development of international economic markets also increasingly raise the game for new criminal activities to exploit both the technologies and those international markets. The very technologies that developed to enable multinational corporations to do more business more effectively, now also offer the prospect of globally organized criminal networks focused on exploiting those technologies (Castells 1996).

VENDOR JASON: There were mutations in the viruses. But it was just newbies who saw a bit of code and think, "Oh, well that virus does this" and have a look at it and write a variation and send another one out there. Then there was occasionally a floppy disc would get passed around and it would spread that way. And then there is the malicious terrorist type, I am sure is still there, where using viruses to stealthily gather information because information is big money and valuable now. Now that we are connected and information is big business, it is moving away from more the amateur virus writer to the professional virus writer because it is all an industry.

The virus writer has changed from the amateur to the professional. This vendor recognizes how 'information is big money and valuable'. He identifies a social order centered on a new political economy of information capital. Information is generated by, enhanced through, and relies on technology. Technology and information are decisive tools in generating profits and in appropriating market shares, resulting in capital, information, and high technology being increasingly interdependent. Information is the new economic, cultural, and political asset, and through commodification, is vulnerable to crime. The antivirus industry recognizes the transformation of both information into a 'big business' and virus writers into a criminal industry. Both the antivirus professional and the virus writer focus on and work within this combined information/technology/financial nexus.

This professionalization of virus writers entails their organization into virtual industries, where they share information, services, new techniques, and new technical innovations in order to collaborate on making virus writing simpler, its products harder to detect, and the process more lucrative (Burke and Ryan 2005). They have structured a community with defined roles and specialties, with networked communications protocols, rules of engagement, and even ethics, all focused on sharing and developing technological information (Krebs 2006). The virus writer's actions are not then one of 'dropping out' or rebelling against the information/technology/financial nexus. The virus writer's manipulation and comprehension of technology also entails understanding and operating within the rules of commodities and consumerism (Ross 1995). Indeed, the industry professional negates the virus writer's new acquisition of technical skills, and demeans the virus writer's ability to take advantage of a networked communication system without the application of the proper moral codes. The antivirus industry accuses this newly professionalized virus writer of 'inappropriately' identifying too closely with the code of capitalism by being an immoral technological thief who endangers business information flows. With 'misdirected' entrepreneurial codes, the immoral and stigmatized professional 'cyber thief' is portrayed by antivirus professionals as comprehending all too well the values inherent within the networked communication system.

The antivirus professional's representation of the virus writer thus points to the complex relationships between knowledge, power, and technology. The antivirus professional's negotiations over the meaning of the computer virus writer is about the realization of power, about issues of technological and economic domination and control, and about the moral premises that differentiate good from bad, all contributing to the definition of threats infiltrating networked information technologies.

Threats, Power, and the State

Beck also contends that negotiations inherent within the 'risk society' have political consequences since "averting and managing these can include a reorganization of power and authority" (Beck 1999, 4). Antivirus professionals want a reorganization of power and authority to better support the corporate development of e-commerce. However, most antivirus professionals see governments as unprepared to preside over the information society. Indeed, antivirus professionals continually assert that there is a need for fundamental transformation surrounding law and technology, and the authority to deal with secrecy and mobility. They see the law as confounded by notions of (dis)embodiment in virtual space, and governments being unable to trans-nationally track information or prosecute a body when their physical presence is dispersed hundreds or even thousands of miles around the world. The ambiguous nature of information, ownership, and the location of bodies in space are practical issues that computer virus writers exploit. Many antivirus professionals see law enforcement and government officials as unable to come to terms with the exploitation of this ambiguity:

RESEARCHER CHARLES: Most law enforcement agencies do not have the understanding of the way the technology is working to be able to address it. The bad guys are pretty mobile; in other words they can move their connections around very quickly. So the greatest risk at the moment is the government's failure to understand this threat. That is a big problem. Governments have their own networks to protect, have their citizens to protect. If people within government could see the threat as we see it, they wouldn't be sitting down doing nothing, which is what they are doing. To a large extent it is an 'emperor's new clothes' scenario that law enforcement don't understand it, and don't want to admit they don't understand it, haven't got people who can help them. So they look the other way.

Antivirus professionals continually lament that governments and law enforcement do not have the ability to effectively pursue and prosecute internet crime. The 'emperor's new clothes' analogy highlights the collective ignorance attributed to those with the power to make a difference, and is compared with the 'truer vision' of the antivirus expert. Governments fail to understand or take appropriate action, despite the seemingly obvious evidence before them. The internet economy and structure is vulnerable, but 'the greatest risk at the moment' is the government's shared group-think, based on outdated and irrelevant conceptualizations of both the problem and appropriate solutions. Antivirus professionals continually expose the limitations of the law, and how commonly accepted notions of law and order have become inadequate and immaterial, but are maintained in spite of the transformations occurring. Within this conceptualization of government inadequacies, the industry provides the necessary service to counter the effects of the technologically literate and immoral virus writer.

Threats and the Antivirus Expert

It is this computer-literate aspect of the virus writers, and their ability to exploit technology and the law, that generates a symbiotic relationship between the computer virus writer and the antivirus professional. Indeed, the antivirus professionals point out many conjoint relationships between themselves and the malicious code writer. This linkage is recognized as supporting the growth of each. A vendor discusses that creative symbiosis:

> VENDOR LEE: I would say that creators, the virus writers, are getting smarter and smarter. They are bound to cause you problems if they attack you psychologically. So like the Mothers' Day Virus, or they impersonate Symantec, or Microsoft, as if they are the technical support people. So it is a cat-and-mouse race that in Chinese we say, "The police's skill is just higher than the thief's highest skill." It is always like that, you must be more skillful. It is always like that, so in this industry, it's about that.

Within the information society, more and more advanced computer skills are required to produce computer viruses, as well as detect and counter them. This collaborative development contributes to the evolution of the 'thief's highest skill'. Electronic vandals continually adapt in response to both technological transformations and the countermeasures of the antivirus industry.

One strategy used by antivirus researchers to ascertain the skill sets of the 'thieves' is to troll the virus writers' underground virtual communities, bulletin boards, and Web sites, interacting with hackers, spammers, and virus code writers. Within these underground communities the antivirus researchers disguise their identities and pretend to be malicious code writers themselves, questioning and discussing malicious code writers' current exploits. The lack of culturally specific embodied identities inherent in the electronic communication of the internet allows these researchers to mask their 'real-world' intentions in their virtual re-embodiment as malware-writing criminals.

Another strategy used by the antivirus industry to ascertain the new techniques and tools of virus writers is the analysis of malware samples sent by infected customers. Significantly, virus writers also send their new creations to various antivirus vendors and researchers as a way of testing vendors' systems, as a 'courtesy', or as a way of marking their status. Antivirus professionals take this information and share it across competitive vendor boundaries, developing industry-wide counterstrategies to be integrated into their next software releases.

The antivirus industry and the virus writers are densely interconnected, their techniques, innovations, and IT artifacts co-evolving within and through the various reactive social and technical communities. Although this co-evolution is recognized, the antivirus industry constructs virus writers as the 'other', as criminal, as thieves, as the 'bad guys'. This 'othering' process makes possible the homogenization of the antivirus professional as the collective 'we' (Hall 1991). Even though the antivirus industry recognizes it has much in common with the virus writers, it still articulates a moral distinctiveness from virus writers, a distinctiveness that gives form to the industry's identity. Referring to both this reciprocity and their distinctive identity, one researcher uses a sword and shield analogy to highlight the sense of continual threat and its effect on the industry:

> RESEARCHER WILLIAM: They are kind of the sword and we are the shield. And when the sword develops, the shield is altered. Unfortunately in most cases, most parts, we are actually reactive, because of new threats. We are trying to investigate new possible threats. But the software industry is so huge, AV cannot possibly cover all of it!

Cat and mouse, police and thief, sword and shield. The analogies are seemingly oppositional, yet also imply reciprocity and integration. The 'bad guy' development of new technological threats generates new risk management techniques. The antivirus industry compensates with new technological solutions that stimulate new threats. There is the assumption within these cyclical analogies that technological developments will always be threatened, that new countermeasures will always be needed in an endless growth cycle of oppositional stimulations. The sense of a never-ending threat is also part of the foundational grounding of the antivirus industry identity, as it responds to and continually differentiates itself from the virus writer. Indeed, the antivirus industry's professional identity is shaped through the lens of threats. Society and technology are continually under attack, continually under siege. It is their job to react to and protect network communications.

As this researcher also suggests, the antivirus industry cannot cover all possible threats to networked information. Antivirus is only part of the larger computer security industry. The continual ever-changing requirements to develop more technology in order to protect the latest technology from the always evolving threats contributes to the proliferation of several other computer security professional specializations: spam filtering, intrusion prevention systems (IPS), access control, network security, firewalls, intrusion detection, and credit card and identity theft, all with their own expert knowledges and corresponding institutions.

Consequently, the 'we' of antivirus is also distinguished from other computer security knowledge systems. The production of professional security knowledge is a key component constituting and regulating the professional(ized) security field within which there is a struggle for resources, reputation, and recognition. The result is a narrow framework within which each professional segment looks at a threat and its solution in relative isolation from the larger systemic causes and consequences. Security knowledge becomes a site of contestation as the antivirus industry's knowledge competes with other technological knowledge systems in an ongoing delineation of boundaries between these various computer security fields. A corporate end user of a large international bank commented upon his use of antivirus software as part of his overarching corporate security infrastructure:

CORPORATE END USER EARL: The AV industry see themselves as something different. And they're really a small component of the whole of the security infrastructure. I've been involved with security for fifteen-odd years, and antivirus is, in theory, a small part of it. Occasionally it becomes a major part of my day-to-day work simply because viruses have that sort of ability to completely consume your time, because if there's an outbreak you simply have to deal with it. Many areas you can say, "Right, well I'll put that off and do it the next day or the day after that." But viruses you can't do that. You have to deal with it there and then. It can be all-consuming. But percentage wise, it's probably only five to ten percent of my time normally.

The antivirus industry is portrayed as seeing itself as 'something different' within the computer security infrastructure, as dividing itself off from the rest of the computer security infrastructure. The antivirus industry's seemingly conscious segmentation and declaration of its uniqueness is both simultaneously accepted and denigrated by this fifteen-year veteran of computer security. He minimizes the antivirus component of his overall computer security focus as only taking up five to ten percent of his time. However, he also identifies the catastrophic all-consuming nature when a virus outbreak occurs. Even though antivirus is only a minor player within computer security, the all-consuming potential catastrophe of a virus outbreak generates the need for and importance of the antivirus industry as part of his entire computer security package.

The threat of a catastrophic technological virus crisis is central to the workings and identity of the antivirus industry. Indeed, an epidemic outbreak can either empower or diminish the authority of the antivirus professional by assigning responsibility for the success or failure of crisis prevention and risk management. A corporate end user of another large multinational corporation discussed the increase in his ability to implement future risk management strategies after an outbreak in his corporation. Because security costs money, it is always negotiated between the perceived costs of various forms of insecurity and their consequences. For him, the 'urgency' of the crisis became a 'tool', providing him with more influence, authority, and financial support. This corporate end user gets 'heard' because he recognizes the negotiation process inherent within an outbreak, and can 'get things done' because of the increased anxiety and stress surrounding the crisis:

CORPORATE END USER EDWARD: Executives control the budget and they also control the urgency in which you can get programs implemented. And that is a powerful tool. Executives control the urgency. If you had a budget that was a million and the immediate problem struck today, okay, that budget could be increased to five million in this quarter. And I have heard people say, "Whatever it costs, write the check." In times of emergency, with that kind of support coming from high up, it's easier to get things done.

I: So do the crises give you power?

CORPORATE END USER EDWARD: Definitely, definitely, if you are there to solve them. You put your ass in a sling if not.

Crises change power relationships. In a technological crisis, money and power are funneled to the IT manager who is held personally responsible for the solution. The person with the technological knowledge is granted more authority and more control, which co-opts the day-to-day battles over the other costs of security.

CORPORATE END USER KENNETH: The last outbreak just went nuts here at [Company Name].

I: What was your job like then when everything went nuts?

CORPORATE END USER KENNETH: Very good! Because I have been saying that we should have it all automated and that all the updates should be automated and I've been working on that and plugging that one for a while. And that got me heard by a few committees that said, "Right, do it." So I've done it.

IT managers exist within the power relationships structured through and by the risk management of a vulnerable yet crucial technological system. During a crisis, the urgency of a virus outbreak can bestow power. However, that power can be a double-edged sword. Another researcher discussed the variability of the power relationships surrounding the 'typical IT security manager':

RESEARCHER THOMAS: When everything runs smoothly no one pays attention to him, his recommendations, or whatever, no one bothers. But when something really bad happens, like a new virus or whatever, they get the blame.

Many antivirus professionals retold this story of the typical IT security manager who cannot control the individuals within the corporate environment. This composite IT manager is at the mercy of the corporation's employees' lack of computer literary and 'idiocy', from the lowly secretary or student who continually reinfects the entire system, to the corporate president who double-clicks and corrupts the entire business network. The IT manager is expected to control and master the technology, in spite of human errors.

It is a paradoxical feature of the practical management of threats that 'success' can be assessed in terms of something not happening, evaluations based on the nonoccurrence of unwanted events that the risk management policy is designed to minimize. The corporate IT manager can be rendered invisible and silenced when outbreaks are successfully averted and in effect become non-events. The IT manager can also be held personally responsible when crises do erupt. Yet, the successful management of risks can also grant the IT manager legitimation and authority, often turning risk management strategies into powerful options and positive visibility.

Crises then create fragmentary effects. Crises can diminish authority, assigning blame and liability. Crises can also elevate and legitimate, raising profiles and setting new technologies in motion. A crisis then has the power to reveal the disparate plurality of responses in which technologies and identities are set into operation, concretely implemented and transformed.

Significantly, the antivirus industry cultivates and markets both this fragmentation and the industry's identity through providing solution-based commodities as the remedy. The industry's power and legitimacy come from adeptly predicting and successfully handling crises. As discussed above, corporate executives, IT committees, and the fifteen-year computer security veteran turn to and rely upon the applied expertise of the antivirus industry during an 'outbreak' or crisis. The effective successful IT manager is represented as adroitly implementing antivirus software on corporate systems. If individual competence and the ability to manage security and technology is demonstrated, the IT manager is then granted status, prestige, and financial clout.

Thus, success is defined and promoted by the antivirus industry as resolving the fragmentary effects of a crisis in three ways: First and foremost, the safety of corporate information is secured; second, IT managers receive the benefits and kudos for successfully securing the safety of that corporate information; and third, failure, which results in the loss of both secure information and job clout, can be averted through antivirus software. The antivirus industry achieves success by shrewdly cultivating insecurities, promoting worst-case scenarios, and adroitly resolving these crises with new technical insights and product innovations.

The power relationships surrounding urgency become fundamental tools of control and personal and financial gain. The motive of both professional malicious code writers and internet providers is centered through manipulating information for profit; 'information is big business'. The intertwined nature of commerce and technology structure both legal and illegal endeavors. According to antivirus professionals, the entangled structures have proved difficult for governments to understand and control. The antivirus industry's suggested solution to securing the internet and regulating internet traffic for legitimate businesses is not to rely on governments, but to purchase and apply its technological innovations and products. Since governments cannot be relied upon, the market and its inherent profit orientation are suggested as the best 'drivers' to protect against unsanctioned uses of the internet. In this sense, the need and solutions for managing threats to the internet have both technical and commercial dimensions that are mutually constitutive and inseparable.

Threats and Commodification

There is an inflationary logic inherent in the commodification of urgency and crises (Ericson and Haggerty 1997; Loader 1999). Consumer capitalism has an extraordinary capacity to take what directly threatens it and convert it into a marketing opportunity. The new technologies generated by the need to manage risk stimulate further demands for protection. Although antivirus technologies are sold on the basis of preventing intrusion and increasing safety, the interactions and relationships developed through servicing risk ultimately generate more products, more dependent relationships, and the perception of more threats to be alleviated.

> VENDOR MARK: Any technology that can be absorbed into the AV product, the corporates want us to do that because they already have our products. We've always had this notion that, once you get into AV, you can never get out. People come to depend on you. It's a trust issue. They want to deal with the same people that they've dealt with in the past.

You develop certain technical capabilities of interpretation, of diagnosis, of doing risk assessments. And because it's a trust relationship, and they see what you've done in the past, they come back to you and ask your opinion on this next thing, and on this next thing, and what can you do to alleviate this next problem. [They ask] "Even if it's not your problem today, can you do something about it?" So that makes everything become a growth into AV.

'The corporates' want to deal with people they trust, with vendors they can rely on to manage their technological risks. An antivirus product becomes an enveloping technological and knowledge system, a system that is a regular inducement to manage the even bigger threats of tomorrow. Corporate end users are portrayed as ensnared within a symbiotic reciprocal cycle from which they cannot escape, because "once you get into AV you can never get out." The antivirus industry forms a kind of 'knowledge monopoly', accumulating clout and turning that clout into a selling point that creates a culture of dependency surrounding that expertise.

The antivirus industry's evolution is embedded within both the demands of transnational corporations' networked security and the innovations and motives of the malicious code writers. In this sense, instead of viewing malicious code writers as potential annihilators of the information society, they can also be seen as an integral and productive part of a capital enterprise, stimulating the development of the antivirus industry to produce more security commodities. In response to crises and threats, the antivirus industry becomes a dynamic system, seemingly able to expand and innovate without relinquishing its specialized expertise. The technological transformations constantly occurring within the industry are created in response to the innovations of virus writers, and are developed in collaboration with the evolving corporate threats and needs of the corporate end users, resulting in the generation of solution-specific innovations. Corporate end users come back to their antivirus vendors, requesting they alleviate the next problem, the next threat. The computer antivirus product thus is woven within the dense and complex practices of the social circulation of risk logic and risk management, shaping and shaped by the new economy of protecting information capital.

The irony is that in the attempts to manage and find solutions to the threats and crises of computer viruses, new risks can be created. Early in the interviews, Microsoft was continually criticized for both the lack of security in its products, and also, its attempts to fix those same security holes. Antivirus professionals continually suggested the fixes created by Microsoft generated further risks.

> CORPORATE END USER STEVEN: I have this healthy disregard for things from Microsoft and essentially the things that Microsoft comes out with. If it comes out with a service pack that has been in service for a long time, it has been tested. Probably it's fairly safe to use. But when they come out with a vulnerability that has just been found yesterday, or last week, or whatever, it's essentially a hot fix. Okay, it's a hot fix. So is it going to work and do what? It may fix the problem, but it may make another. And it may not even completely fix the problem.

In the early days of the antivirus industry, Microsoft was renowned for its inability to supply secure software, and for incompetently compensating for breaches of that security. Microsoft's processes and techniques of risk management became the producer of new risks. The expert knowledge and technological innovations used to fix security holes became the source of other risks and fodder for the antivirus industry. Because of this type of pressure, Microsoft is slowly improving the security in its products and the reliability of its patches.

A key feature of the risk logic in the information age is the instability of its core networking technology and its chronic dependence on continual security upgrades to patch new vulnerabilities. Paradoxically, while risk logic is based on threats and dangers, it can also be seen as resulting in productive effects. The criminal tactics stir new growth areas of commodity production, manifested not only in the burgeoning expansion of the computer security industry, but equally in the appropriation and subsequent dependency of corporate security infrastructures on that security industry. The required circulation of 'free-flowing' and frictionless information is secured through the necessary production of new technologies, new industries, and new power relationships.

The antivirus industry, as both a knowledge industry and technological profession, produces a commodity to manage and regulate one aspect of network vulnerability. Network vulnerability is explained through embodied metaphors of biological viruses and threats of widespread epidemics, grounding the threat in a larger culture of fear, health scares, and biological virus outbreaks. The threats to the network communication system are represented as enacted by immoral and evolving professional virus writers, who are technically savvy and deeply immersed within a transnational consumer culture. The identity of the antivirus industry is based on responding to this specific technological threat and preventing a catastrophic outbreak or epidemic by applying high-tech research and commodifying that research into specialized competitive innovations.

Protection is informational, grounded in the productivity of industry professionals, who also fundamentally depend upon their capacity to generate, process, and efficiently apply knowledge-based information within the competitive corporate marketplace. Their technological innovations are focused on securing corporate assets. The very process of protecting those assets is integral to the identity of, and need for, the antivirus industry, in effect, establishing and reaffirming the industry's identity. The visibility of antivirus technology becomes significant in that the locus of controlling virus writers defaults to the marketplace because governments and the police are seen as unwilling or unable to provide that protection. Thus, protecting the internet is not just a technological issue. It is a fragmented and competitive organizational process that distributes information, generates knowledge and expertise, transforms power relationships, and promotes the need for antivirus software products to protect a vulnerable information society.

2 Security Transformations

The Security/Threat Dichotomy

The standard definition of security circulating within the antivirus industry is protecting 'CIA'—the Confidentiality, Integrity, and Availability of data, projects, or services. This chapter complicates this definition. 'Security' is not a neutral fact, not merely a techno-instrumental or managerial orientation, not a word or state of being that is universally understood. Within the antivirus industry, contradictory interpretations of 'security' expose the fears surrounding the global flows of information and the conflicting identities within the industry. This chapter analyzes how concerns for, and uses of security underpin, animate, and reinforce forms of power, identity, and economic circulation within the industry.

Definitions of security always suggest the tacit assumption of 'threat' (Burke 2002; Weldes 1999). In the interviews, when people were asked what does security mean, they largely specified the 'facts'; how security might be attained; and what might be the most basic, effective, or cost-effective means of doing so. Throughout this interviewing process a security paradox developed; security was never mentioned without also identifying the threat to that security. One always occurred with the other. When discussing security issues, what needed to be secured was

identified as threatened. Note how the researcher quoted below conflates security, risk, and threat in his response to the question about his
definition of security:

> I: How do you define 'security'?
>
> RESEARCHER KEITH: Security is about risk management, not
> risk prevention, risk management. The way to view security
> is as risk management. Risk is a tricky issue in its own right.
> There are various models of how you try and make sense of
> that from a business perspective. But security in the sense
> that I talk about it is really about risk management.
>
> I: How do you define 'risk'?
>
> RESEARCHER KEITH: Um, I'm trying to remember . . . the
> most common of these definitions is a simple little formula
> which is: risk equals threat, multiplied by exposure. Then
> you have to define what threat is [laughs].

This researcher's entwined discussion of security, risk, and threat
nicely captures the substantive assumption underlying this chapter,
namely that security, risk, threat, and insecurity are all mutually constitutive, each referencing each other. Seemingly contradictory, the
value of security relies on and is dependent upon, the threat it claims
to manage, supersede, or expel (Krause and Williams 1997). That is,
security only exists in relation to a threat. Security is not an absolute
objective state in and of itself.

The idealized state of securing total confidentiality, integrity, and
availability of data is impossible. No system or network can be utilized
and simultaneously completely protected from threats.[1] All antivirus
professionals agree that with sufficient motivation, resources, and ingenuity an individual can compromise the most sophisticated of security
safeguards. The question then becomes how can optimum security be
achieved.

---

[1] Eugene Spafford, professor of computer science and electrical and computer engineering and historically revered for his contributions to internet security, is attributed the following aphorism: "The only system which is truly secure is one which is
switched off and unplugged, locked in a titanium lined safe, buried in a concrete
bunker, and is surrounded by nerve gas and very highly paid armed guards. Even

VENDOR JASON: The easiest way not to get infected is not to turn your computer on. But there has to be a balance between what is practical and what is safe. And if you don't give anyone control, then not as much gets done. Obviously it's a question of who has control.

As this vendor articulates, security is a compromise. It is a negotiation between practicality and safety. What 'gets done' must be 'balanced' against security issues. However, this balance is an issue of power and relationships, a 'question of who has control'. Security in this sense is not an 'essence' in and of itself, it is not an individualized or subjective state of being. It is a value negotiated with others. It is contested in daily interactions as people work with and apply the security and practicality compromises.

The Costs of Antivirus Security

The optimum security policy is one in which the costs of implementing protective mechanisms, including usability, functionality, and financial assessments of the threats, are balanced against the reduction in risk. Antivirus vendors must take this negotiated, balanced, and secured state into account when working with their corporate customers. As one corporate end user stated:

CORPORATE END USER CHRIS: In something as critical as our security infrastructure, it is important [Antivirus Vendor] work with us. Because security is the bottom line. And if you're not working with us, then you're not the vendor for us.

Chris, an IT manager in a large transnational corporation, identifies security as the bottom line of his business operations. He evaluates antivirus vendors based on their ability to understand and work within his company's security structure. Those who cannot work within his

---

then, I wouldn't stake my life on it." There is also the much shorter "Richards' Laws of Computer Security"—1st Law: Don't buy a computer. 2nd Law: If you do buy a computer, don't turn it on.

seemingly unique usability and security framework are rejected as antivirus security providers. Security as the 'bottom line' becomes Chris's way of ranking or evaluating antivirus vendors.

Both Jason as a vendor, and Chris as a corporate end user, articulate a symbolic logic, what some would call the 'grammar' of the security formation. Both discuss the importance of security in relationship to other people. Jason identifies the control issues that must be negotiated between how safe the system is and a system's usability or functionality for the end user. Chris, as a corporate end user, rejects antivirus vendors that do not work alongside his company's interpretation of the security/functionality ratio. Both Jason and Chris articulate how business and working relationships are constructed through the value of security.

Security is thus entrenched in institutionalized patterns of other daily practices. When the vendor and the corporate end user talk about security, they reveal a pervasive and complex system of political, social, and economic power relationships. These quotes suggest that security is not a 'universality', but a field of conflict that emerges in the negotiations over threats to technological priorities in the compromises and interactions of daily contacts. Security becomes a form of technological discipline through that negotiation process.

Government and Security Discourses

As the above quotes suggest, security occupies a key enabling position at the junction of technology and the economy. How much work is produced and constrained, and the evaluation or elimination of a commercial antivirus vendor, are all negotiated through a security discourse. The state is also an integral partner in this economic and technocratic negotiation over security, deriving enormous cultural power from its role of 'protecting the people'. In a pluralist notion of the state, the state is charged with arbitrating between the competing interests of the 'private person', including both individuals and corporations, and 'the public'—an abstract, collective identity reduced to a set of assumed shared interests (Bigo 2002). The state is constructed as the 'neutral arbiter' that can mediate the competing interests, protecting private persons when appropriate, and protecting the public from certain kinds of persons, such as criminals and terrorists.

This interpretation of the state as neutral arbiter protecting the people was articulated by many within the antivirus industry from both Eastern and Western nation–states.

> VENDOR GEORGE: In China, People's Republic of China, antivirus is a national defense business. Although it is an industry like any other commercial industry, but that is all controlled by the government. All the outside and even inside. I mean the local antivirus development software, they all have to go past the central public supporting ministry for antivirus decisions in order to prove. . . . [The public minister] would say, "You talk about finding 1,000 viruses, prove it to me. Give me your software. Come to our lab even. Give me the data. Show me the virus that you can detect." In China's central lab, the government lab will say, "We will test this, what you say. If you prove to achieve what you said, then we give you accreditation that you can sell in China," which is very valuable.

> RESEARCHER WILLIAM: The recent progress into taking botnets off servers when they are found means that [botmasters] are going to concentrate on making them more difficult to find. That's going to carry on until there is some form of penalty, legal penalty for that type of activity. But so far, only one government has taken it seriously, that is Australia.

The Chinese and Australian governments are depicted as protectors of the public, properly defending their citizens. In this view, the provision of technological security is entrusted to the state, with the assumption that the government should actively guard its citizens from threats emanating from unethical or dangerous elements, whether they be computer viruses, unscrupulous vendors, or bot-masters. Technological security and protection of the internet is promoted through implementation of state-sanctioned policy, surveillance, and laws.

Such representations originate from the assumed governmental power to provide solutions and eliminate threats. Many antivirus professionals consider the state as fundamentally responsible for identifying technological threats and providing internet security, even as many others critique the state's ineffectual application. In their negotiations with government officials over protecting the internet, the concept of security is used by antivirus professionals as the evaluative marker to measure the success or failure of legislators and law officers. Police and politicians are assessed positively and negatively on their ability to enforce and to legislate technological security. Indeed, it is through their interaction with state authorities that antivirus professionals assert their place within that social order, claiming their status as security and technology experts over and above most governmental officials. Security is a tactical and discursive power essential to the identity of the antivirus industry and promoted by these professionals as the highest priority within a technocratic society.

The porous nature of, and lack of national boundaries on, the internet makes regulating and disciplining international web-based industries and private sector organizations complex and difficult. Understanding this, most in the antivirus industry recast the concept of policing and prosecuting as an international concern that requires the coordinated efforts of multiple nation–states. The need to protect cyberspace demands an extension of and coordination between the policing function of all states. The majority of people interviewed both critiqued the current status of governmental efforts at countering international malware practices and supported the extension of international coordination.

> VENDOR BRIAN: I want to see more consolidation of laws against electronic warfare, against virus writing as well. I want consistent laws between countries so that the virus writers don't feel safe in any of the countries. So, I want virus writing to be outlawed uniformly everywhere.

> RESEARCHER THOMAS: I would like to see harsher penalties for those people who are caught. I would like to see some changes in internet protocols so that there is more, a better identity so that we can track things internationally.

Though current prosecution of internet crimes is still seen as deficient, antivirus professionals welcome international coordination as representing the interests of networked global security. Electronic warfare and virus writing are conflated into one criminal act, needing more cooperation and transnational legislation. The vendor above would like virus writers to be uniformly outlawed. The researcher would like changes in both internet protocols and criminal penalties. He would like to make the identities of all end users around the world more visible in order to better monitor, track, and prosecute networked criminals. These statements articulate dissatisfaction with current technical protocols and legislative procedures, and a desire for international surveillance and uniform punishment 'everywhere'.

Computer Security and Cyber Terrorism after 9/11

After 9/11 the antivirus industry increased its cooperation with both domestic and international government agencies and those agencies' definitions of security. Some antivirus professionals worked directly with Homeland Security in the United States and the Home Office in the United Kingdom. A U.S.-based vendor states:

> VENDOR GARY: In both France and the United Kingdom, I think they've certainly stepped up their efforts to, you know, prosecute and try to find people. We just had a researcher the last month do a testimony to what's called the Home Office in the United Kingdom about a virus to help them put, what do you call it? . . . a prosecution . . . , a case together against someone in the United Kingdom, to successfully prosecute the person. So they certainly have stepped up what they're doing. France had always been diligent from what I can tell in this area. I think that they've probably escalated some things themselves. We have someone that works with the French authorities almost on a weekly basis and they have stepped up their protection themselves on what they do, to make sure that they're secure.

Another U.S.-based vendor discusses the role of the U.S. government:

VENDOR LOU: I don't think that our company was affected by September 11th directly. I think most of the changes were coming from the government because the government started to bring forth whatever security measures they have. They tried to implement new security measures like the Homeland Security . . . they started this big project. And that's where I see the effects coming from. We are basically just reacting to the government, to whatever the government has pushed onto us. But I'm talking about the U.S., not from any other county.

After 9/11, some within the antivirus industry became participants in international state-sponsored activities, providing domestic and international technical advice and evidence. The United States, United Kingdom, and French prioritization of security seem compatible with the antivirus industry's priorities. However, as the last quote implies, many within the industry consider state-oriented security discourses as being 'pushed' on to the industry, that the antivirus industry is 'basically just reacting to the government'. Significantly, the direct and residual effects of 9/11 were largely insignificant to the people interviewed. Security was separated into various categories, and cyber terrorism was discounted as a nonthreat:

RESEARCHER WILLIAM: Cyber terrorism is a marketing ploy. Um, it's a buzzword that's certain . . . mainly political, and that some businesspeople use to scare funding out of mostly the U.S. government and its agencies, mainly for imagined and hypothetical but very, very distant 'threats'.

VENDOR GEORGE: Homeland Security, that's just a big marketing effort to convince people to give up their rights for the sake of this illusory threat, which doesn't exist really, you know.

In a post-9/11 world, much media and political discourse centers on terror networks, techno-war, civilian casualties, and the need to create an international system focused on achieving more comprehensive security. The United States, in particular, has made a point of defining security against terrorism as the overarching value for the entire world, as a way of building a military-based network that prioritizes security over other 'lesser' goals. Because of the mediated national security discourses associated with 9/11, I had assumed the antivirus industry would also be espousing state-sanctioned cyber-terrorism threats.

The U.S. government, however, is not the only site for the production of security discourses. Beyond the United States' narrowly defined security discourses there are other institutions that produce and circulate their version of security. Indeed, the majority of antivirus professionals flatly reject real connections between the antivirus industry, 9/11, and any of the resulting legislation or world events. Through their own media analysis, the majority of the interviewees directly challenged the U.S. government's presumed exclusive privilege to define and interpret 9/11 as contributing to a 'cyber threat'. They critiqued the mystique surrounding 'national security' and did not accept cyber terrorism as a clear and present, or even 'real', danger.

The significance of this process, though, is how the objects of threat in the so-called 'war on terror' are critiqued by the antivirus industry.

> VENDOR GEORGE: The really bad thing about all that is it seems to be using the excuse of the war against terrorism to pull, to grab control, or to try to grab control of lots of things and things that they shouldn't be getting into. It probably isn't too long before pirating a music file is international terrorism.

> RESEARCHER MICHAEL: The only difference was that before 9/11 everybody was talking about China. After 9/11, or immediately after 9/11, the concentration went over to Al Qaeda. But after recognizing that Al Qaeda didn't pose a threat there, everybody went back to China.

Questioning computer security issues surrounding 9/11 generates critiques of security definitions and the impact on technological infrastructures. The war on terror is seen as merely an excuse to assert untenable authority. The technical viability of the state-sanctioned security issues, whether they be pirating music, Al Qaeda, or China, are questioned and seen to be inconsistent.

Antivirus professionals' interactions with government officials are thus conflicted. Some of these professionals rely on the state to be a 'neutral arbiter' and national security provider, yet others continually critique and challenge the state for its failure to understand, identify, legislate, and enforce appropriate international technological security. Expectations and social exchanges between government and the antivirus industry are negotiated through the rank that technological security prioritizes. For the antivirus industry, these priorities and values suggest industry-specific targets and solutions, draw lines of affiliation and distance between 'us' and various categories of 'them', and attribute blame for malware proliferation. Defining security is thus an exercise in social power, signifying conflicts in status hierarchies and identities.

Case Study: The Transformation of Spam into a Security Threat

The process of calibrating danger, negotiating security, and defining threat can be seen in the transformation of spam. Spam began as a mere annoyance and minor inconvenience in the late 1980s and grew in volume and significance until today it has the potential to perilously obstruct the flow of internet commerce through the botnets of proxy and 'zombie' machines sending billions of unsolicited bulk e-mails. The antivirus industry must negotiate these changes in new threats. They must adapt to and anticipate the fluid transformations of the technological infrastructure, while also negotiating the continually evolving relationships with the state and other computer security providers. A researcher states his definition of spam:

> RESEARCHER CHARLES: A spammer says, "Spam is that which we do not do." ISPs say, "Spam is what our customers do not do." But it's very simple. Spam is a message, sent electronically, in bulk, which the recipient has neither asked for nor given consent for.

While this may seem like a simple straightforward definition of spam, it also reveals the contestation over the applicability of that definition. Spammers and the internet service provider's (ISP) customers might agree with this researcher's definition of electronic bulk mail, but this researcher also suggests they would disagree that their actions could be defined as spam, and would debate definitions of recipient requests and consent. This recognition of various socially-situated definitions is important in order to highlight how the power relations within the antivirus industry affect the negotiations over the implementation of technical security issues.

Interviews conducted in 2003 illustrated the still competing and contradictory calibrations surrounding the antivirus industry's definition of the threat posed by spam.

I: How do you define 'threat'?

RESEARCHER DANIEL: Hmm. That's a really difficult question. Well, how do you define 'annoyance'? A threat is something that can cause really serious damage to a victim. I mean not as a mass victim but a single victim, maybe related to physical injury and possible loss of human life and so on. Also physical damage to a building or something like that, this is what I would call a threat. Spam? No. It's just filling your mailbox. This is not a threat. It's an annoyance.

I: Is spam a security issue?

VENDOR MARK: Most certainly, yes. Since it involves large volumes of data being e-mailed. It is a form of denial of service in a similar way that mass-mailing viruses are: The availability of the legitimate data may be compromised.

The 'risk' of spam is dependent upon the calibration of potential damage to secure systems. Both the researcher and vendor above would agree that an annoyance does not jeopardize systems. Spam is defined as an annoyance when it 'just fills your mailbox'. As anthropologist Mary Douglas suggests, a risk is not a 'thing' but a way of thinking—"not only the probability of an event but also the probable magnitude of its outcome, and everything depends on the value that is set on the outcome" (Douglas 1992, 31). In the case of spam, the outcome in 2003 was considered either a mere annoyance or a substantial threat to the 'A' in CIA—the 'Availability' of legitimate data.

In order to rank dangers, there must be some agreement on criteria, which is why negotiations of security are always political issues. According to Douglas, a modern society organizes danger through institutions that play a central role in the production and regulation of particular dangers. This production and regulation of the spam danger-calibrations can be observed in the next quote from a corporate manager in 2004. *Virus Bulletin* is the only computer security industry journal specializing in both virus and antivirus issues and is highly regarded in this respect. A corporate manager discusses his surprise that *Virus Bulletin* began to include articles on spam:

> CORPORATE END USER CHRIS: I must admit I was a bit taken aback when I saw the huge focus on spam in *Virus Bulletin*. But the more I think about it, the more it makes sense. As I work closely with the messaging organization at my company, I am very much tied into the spam problem. BUT, more importantly, it appears that virus writers are utilizing some spamming techniques, and the best example was SoBig. I see more and more the integration of spam and malware. It is a good way for the malware to get wide distribution. Therefore, AV and spam tools can be integrated. We actually use a multilayered approach for our spam problem, just as we do with the virus world, and yet we still have a spam problem! If virus writers utilized some of these techniques, and some are, we could have huge problems in store for us. I would have to say that it makes sense to integrate these technologies.

This corporate manager was initially surprised at *Virus Bulletin's* focus on spam. However, his calibration of the risk factors associated with spam have changed, reflecting the new technological integration of malware with spam. Spam is no longer a mere annoyance but a new technological vehicle used to distribute malware more effectively. He now sees spam to be a danger, closely allied and entwined with the increased threat of malware to his security infrastructure. The calibration of the probable magnitude of entwined malware–spam outcome, his worst-case scenario, expands the spam threat potential. Because of this, he concludes that *Virus Bulletin* was correct in adding a section on spam.

The entwined malware–spam danger discourses, cemented in a widely respected journal, then provide direction, guidance, knowledge, and new technologies through which all interested industry professionals, the corporate end users, antivirus vendors, and researchers can take action. *Virus Bulletin* legitimates, and is legitimated by, its inclusion of spam as a 'real' threat.

The initial divergent views of spam's threat potential articulated in 2003 changed as the technological threat of spam evolved with global information flows. With botnets of compromised machines controlled by groups of 'abusers', the internet is increasingly seen as unsafe and insecure. Russian, Nigerian, and American spammers threaten global communications, constructing extensive transnational and hidden networks of zombie machines dedicated to sending their spam messages with their own monetary agendas.

By 2006, the risk attached to the spam threat was articulated in terms of its ability to not only directly affect global information flows, but also to severely compromise the general public's willingness to trust and thus engage in e-commerce. All interviewees agree that spam is no longer merely an annoyance but has the capacity to dramatically impact corporate business operations. Spam's impact could rival that of 9/11.

> RESEARCHER CHARLES: If the fraudsters destroy e-commerce as we know it, and we're starting to rely so much on it, it's going to do us a lot of harm. If the fraudsters undermine the banking system, and there is every indication that they're close to doing that through insecure mirrors and proxies all over the net so you can't see where it's coming from, then in all honesty, that does far more harm than knocking down a couple of towers and the like. No lives are lost, but even so, the overall impact is greater. And we're heading that way. Whether it's caught in time, I don't know. I'm looking at what I see as heading toward a meltdown situation at the moment, simply because the volume of issues out there are far greater than one can handle.

Spam evolved from a mere annoyance to currently compromising the security of the entire globally interconnected internet. The threat is from 'fraudsters' and virus writers who can potentially undermine trust in the electronic banking systems supporting e-commerce. The ability to stymie the world's police forces and antivirus researchers is leading to a 'meltdown', potentially worse than the destruction of 'a couple of towers'.

The antivirus industry is immersed in a volatile and rapidly changing world, mirroring and reflecting the transformations in the information superhighway and its dark alleys. Those transformations affect the shape of the computer security industries as they attempt to protect that highway. One response is the merger of antivirus companies and antispam companies.

> RESEARCHER KEITH: Antispam is a big business now, something that the large corporate customers are prepared to pay for products to reduce the amount of spam that comes into their network, you know, lands in their users' inboxes. So there's money to be made from doing it. The early antispam products were always free or relatively cheap. So there's now money to be made doing it and so antivirus companies tend to be relatively cash-rich. So they've gone out and bought antispam companies. And aside from that, you'll see an increasing convergence, merging of the more general computer security and antivirus functions. Whether that will be in security companies that look like buying or obtaining antivirus technology, or whether it will be antivirus companies buying or obtaining other types of security technology, is a bit of an open question. And it will probably be a bit of both.

When spam was a mere annoyance, antispam software was free. The transformation of spam into a security issue threatening e-commerce generated financial incentives for 'cash-rich' antivirus companies to buy antispam companies. There are now agreements on the definition of spam as a security threat, based on common interests in the management of the similar threats posed by malicious code and spam. Like antivirus software, antispam became an indispensible commodity available for corporations to purchase to protect network flows.

The discourses of danger articulated over spam produce real-world effects. Spam's evolution, from a mere annoyance to a combined malware threat challenging the global economic structure, affects industry journal orientations, new technological innovations, and corporate and industry mergers. The 'threat' of spam is institutionalized, reifying both threat and the need for more security products.

The ranking of potential threats evolves as technology evolves, the antivirus industry adapting to and profiting from these evolving definitions. *Virus Bulletin,* as one of those that circulates and institutionalizes changing security definitions, reported the risk potentials and the criteria for their successful management to its readers. The journal articulated for the antivirus professional, the rules, formats, and narratives for action surrounding spam. *Virus Bulletin* provided an obvious benchmark for its readers, a connection that provided knowledge of security issues and the goals for eradicating the spam threat.

These threat and security discourses make visible how the computer communication infrastructure remains highly vulnerable to intrusion, interference, and disruption, and in some people's opinion, an approaching catastrophe worse than 9/11. These threats proliferate and yet are simultaneously rendered potentially manageable through the dedication of more resources directed toward technological innovation. The combined effect ultimately extends the market for more antivirus and computer security products. Agreement on the definition of spam as a security risk is promoted through the social circuitry of risk communication.

3 Trust, Networks, and the Transformation of Organizational Power

Overview of the Structure of the Antivirus Industry

Any discussion of the social construction of security and threat raises two questions about agency and resistance: first, who are the people who define what is threatened, and second, when is security achieved? The first two chapters focused on the negotiations surrounding various definitions of security and threat articulated within the antivirus (AV) industry. This chapter focuses on how various industry professionals go about legitimating their definitions, and the effect these negotiations have on the products and technological innovations created to manage malicious code.

Most of the professionals interviewed within the antivirus industry defined themselves as high-tech experts with specialist and secret knowledge. Their career perspective is to battle daily, sometimes hourly, against malicious and relatively well-informed virus writers for the power and control of the internet. This 'white hat' versus 'black hat' struggle is over aspects of the same secret knowledge system shared between virus writers and the high-tech antivirus professionals. It is a contest over a hierarchical ordered knowledge structure that is recognized by both as continually and rapidly evolving, but vulnerable to disruption and exploitation.

The social location, however, of all the variously situated industry professionals—the researchers, vendors, and corporate end users who roll out antivirus software at their work sites—calls into question the fundamental premise of a single perspective on a solution to the computer virus problem. The researchers, the vendors, and the corporate end users process different information and are granted different financial benefits and authority. In fact, the antivirus industry differentiates these occupations within a security hierarchy, assigning status to each of them. That hierarchy is continually evolving and continually contested. Technological development within the antivirus industry is a process in which these multiple groups, each embodying a specific orientation to antivirus software, negotiate over its design and implementation, sometimes simultaneously seeking quite different objectives and goals. Strategic battles and casualties ensue.

The antivirus software that is produced from these battles and casualties secures information in specific ways, not only because the software works in some objective sense, but because, through their more successful skirmishes, one social group is better able to effect their position and their perspective on the software (Klein and Kleinman 2002). Through the political struggles and strategic negotiations between antivirus researchers, antivirus vendors, and the corporate end users, antivirus software is produced for and used in the corporate market.[1] This chapter is about CARO, an elite organization of antivirus researchers who once formed a knowledge monopoly within the antivirus industry. This chapter focuses on their struggles and influence over the industry and the challenges to their power.

Computer Antivirus Researchers

CARO is an acronym for the Computer Antivirus Research Organization. Their Web site states that CARO is "an informal group of individ-

---

[1] Although two antivirus vendors place a heavy emphasis on the home market, the home market was not the topic of concern for the antivirus industry during the interview period. These two vendors are also the ones currently perceived to be most at threat from the Microsoft 'advance' into antivirus software, which (at least initially) is widely believed to mainly be an advance into the home and small business market sectors.

uals who have been working together since around 1990 across corporate and academic borders to study the phenomenon of computer malware" (www.caro.org). The Web site describes CARO as a "technical group" and emphasizes its "less formal" status as "a group of individuals who trust one another enough to exchange sensitive information on malware." The web page also has a list of its individual members "who wish to go public." Interestingly, in 2006 there were only seven members listed. In their interviews, CARO members suggested there were approximately twenty-five men and one woman.

Why is it important to an analysis of the antivirus industry that it has an 'informal technical group' of about twenty-five individuals who work "across corporate and academic borders" and "trust" each other enough to "exchange sensitive information"? A vendor explained how these researchers are a separate, almost self-contained, subset of the industry:

> VENDOR RONALD: A traditional software industry or even as a traditional industry in general, I am sure AV is somewhat in a different class because of the cooperation aspects. I mean, I do think that this is a group of people, in terms of [CARO] researchers, [who] are really working towards ridding the world of viruses. It's a different story for the people that they work for, but I think that this is a group, and that they do have a common goal to rid the world of that. In terms of for-profit industry sort of thing, it is probably fairly unique. I mean, you don't have chemical companies like Bristol-Myers getting together and like sharing chemical formulas and sharing like, how you do this. So I think it is somewhat unique in that respect.

Initially I assumed there were the conventional divisions within the antivirus industry—vendors as producers and developers, and their corporate customers. Initially I assumed that the antivirus researchers, as part of a research and development division, were indistinct as a category from their employers as commercial developers of antivirus software.

However, as the quote above suggests, antivirus professionals conceptualize the CARO antivirus researcher as somewhat separate from the rest of the industry.[2] They are 'different', attempting to 'rid the world' of viruses. The researchers connect and cross borders of academic, scientific, corporate, and technical networks. They are seen as the benevolent experts and scientists, the ethical core and foundation of the antivirus industry's unique identity, contributing their time, knowledge, and expertise in order to fight the global dissemination of malicious code. Through their seemingly altruistic good works, the researchers' intentions are juxtaposed and contrasted with both the profit motives of other industry professionals and the immorality and criminality of the malicious code writer. By traversing and cooperating across corporate and academic borders, CARO members become the fundamental resource for supplying, shaping, and guiding the industry's technical innovations.

This mythic portrayal of CARO is important both for what it reveals and for what it conceals. The image of CARO as a community of technology research experts who contribute to the advancement of internet security for the common good of the entire global community glosses over the conflicts, struggles, and divisions within the industry. It depoliticizes and almost purifies the tensions and conflicts surrounding the creation and maintenance of their expert status. What is significant is what the myths mean to the people who produce and believe in them, and what they reveal about the industry that attempts to sustain them through the continual upheaval and transformation of network technology.

Mythic Past

Histories of the internet highlight a constant, multisided, and often uneven and unintentional collaboration between universities, the military, 'big science', and computer countercultures. The historical development of the internet is seen as an autonomous process of research, innovation, and application that developed not as a response to the crisis of industrial capitalism but as the work of a 'community of practice' that emerged at the unlikely crossroads of military-sponsored big science, and university-based countercultural networks (Castells 2001). And these divergent technological cultures continue to mark the evolution

---

[2] All but one of the researchers interviewed within this book are members of CARO.

and use of the internet. The informality and self-directedness of communication is still present. The scholarly tradition of the shared pursuit of science, of reputation by excellence, of peer review, and of openness in all research findings is still present though found in more narrowed enclaves and pursuits. Even if the most heroic tones and the counter-cultural ideology of those early days have faded with their applications in 'techno-capitalism', some of those technological features and social codes, such as the idea that 'many contribute to many' that developed from the cooperative impetus and original free use of the network, can still be found in, for example, the open source movement.

The details of the technological revolution and open source philosophy have been chronicled numerous times, and their presentation is beyond the scope of this chapter.[3] Suffice it to say that histories of the development of the computer suggest the internet is a remarkable example of how technological productivity through cooperation positively transformed the internet itself (Castells 2001; Lessig 1999). The drivers of corporate capitalism emerged later, only after profit could be reliably predicted.

The computer antivirus industry emerged from, and is interwoven within, the 'techno-meritocratic' research and development strategies of the internet, the countercultural impetus, and the corporate for-profit motivation. Early models of self-replicating code began as mathematical problems, and were abstractly developed and played with as intellectual games by an artificial intelligence group at Massachusetts Institute of Technology (MIT). Virus-like programs slowly began creeping out of the computer lab, appearing on microcomputers in the early 1980s. By the late 1980s the computer specialists began to take notice:

> RESEARCHER THOMAS: The year was 19 . . . I can't remember exactly, '87 or '88, or one of those years. I was working in the computer industry, in the software development and research side of the industry. The institution I worked for was a research institution. I was working on some network project. I was working on the remote dispatch from one PC to another. Back then we didn't have the internet, nets.

---

[3] See Wall 2001; Castells 1996, 2001, 2003.

And right in the middle when I was debugging some program of mine, all of a sudden the letters on the screen all started all falling down. So I got, you know, upset. So I started doing the investigation of what might have happened, what was the reason. I had heard about computer viruses at that time already. I had heard of Debug. In about two minutes, I had my first antivirus. The virus itself was of course, what is known as Cascade because it drops the letters. And that's how I got involved. And it appeared to be interesting enough and basically I did this in my free time, I would say. I had another project that I did, but I got more and more involved and it got more and more interesting to me. And then when e-mail became available, I was contacting colleagues, outside [Country Name], conversing with colleagues abroad, I mean everywhere.

This CARO member's entry into the development of antivirus software is typical of most CARO members. The majority had previous higher education connections and were working in some type of computer-related research and development when an example or infection of self-replicating code caught their attention. They began individually investigating viruses, working on detecting and disinfecting viruses in their 'free time'. They enlarged their pool of information through e-mail communication, and through attending and presenting at computer conferences, thus sharing ideas and frustrations. CARO as an informal organization was initiated at a 1990 antivirus conference by this e-group of researchers in order to better pool their information. Through sharing their specialized individual knowledges and exchanging their unique perspectives on file formats, programming, and debugging tips, they all benefited. For example, when Microsoft Word macro viruses appeared, the complex Word file format had to be rapidly and extensively researched and understood. All of these researchers needed to cooperate.

RESEARCHER KEITH: They had a meeting behind the scenes where these people from all these different companies got together and they said, "This is what we know about making sense of the Microsoft Word document format." And they just pooled all their information. Some people would have gone in there with very little information; some would have gone in there with nearly everything. Everyone came out with something that they didn't have before they went in. And so it was worth it to them. It was worth it, doing that. So those sort of things have really, that sort of thing really cements, helped cement those relationships.

Needing to more completely understand the Microsoft Word document format, this group of like-minded individuals met 'behind the scenes' in order to cooperatively troubleshoot and share technical knowledge. CARO is portrayed as having been initiated through personal networks that cut across corporate borders, bringing together the top computer virus researchers from 'all these different companies' to 'pool all their information'. CARO is mythically located at the top of the techno-meritocratic culture of scientific and technological excellence and expertise, united in vision, sharing information, and pitting themselves against computer viruses that exploited Microsoft's insecure operating systems.

Trust—Informational Ethics and Power

At the top of antivirus expertise, CARO members came together, motivated by the need to secure the internet through exchanging virus samples and information about viruses. The need to share information and to collaborate is central to their rationale. Much of their collaborations were focused on deconstructing Microsoft programs, which were continually identified as built for functionality and ease of use, rather than security. Indeed, much of their time was spent reverse-engineering Microsoft programs as they repeatedly suggested Microsoft was unable or unwilling to provide the necessary information. Through sharing their analysis of Microsoft programs and through intense collaboration on the impact viruses had on those programs, they provided the entire computer industry with solutions to both present attacks and future potential outbreaks.

CARO members conducted this research within a threatening environment, where the risk of an outbreak was constant. Identifying who they could trust and knowing with whom they could exchange this sensitive information was critical.

RESEARCHER THOMAS: Your users, they have to be protected. They might have got this virus already. So you have to share virus samples. You have to share virus information with other antivirus people so that on the whole, all the industry becomes more reactive. And that we did back in the early '90s. There were several organizations created, some formal, some completely informal like CARO, for example, which is an organization only by name. It's more like a club, where people do exactly that. Based on the mutual trust you shared information, the tests of the virus sample, other inquiries, working with your competitor. And they do the same for you. It also was very helpful, extremely helpful when cases where antivirus for new applications appeared, where say, some file problem with a Word document was a complete mystery and no one knew what was inside. So it was a cooperative effort back then, with the lack of support from Microsoft.

Microsoft was identified as not providing the antivirus industry information or support to understand their programs and file formats. CARO was needed to protect the users. In the crisis of an outbreak, the urgent need to contain the outbreak, to find an antidote is critical. CARO is the informal organization based on mutual trust where these researchers cooperatively share information, 'working with your competitor' across the industry in order to find solutions. Their joint efforts allowed the industry 'on the whole' to become more reactive, able to find solutions or antidotes for malware infections on new Microsoft applications.

Sharing this information, however, is also problematic. This collaborative effort can only be accomplished among other trusted, thus known, researchers:

RESEARCHER THOMAS: I have to know that this person will not do such a thing, that he himself knows how to safely manage viruses, and trust him with these issues. And then I will readily exchange information. Information is like a double-edged sword. It can be used and it can be misused.

We don't want some of the information we know about the file formats to become available to say, the virus writers.

The danger inherent in the concept of the double-edged sword highlights the need to set boundaries and exclude others from influence over information. It also portrays the CARO member as the gatekeeper of a consistent ethical value system for 'legitimate' antivirus professionals.

As a gatekeeper, this member of CARO emphasizes his authorization and rights of access. Such criteria are held to be fundamental because they stem from the basic belief in his expertise, in his ability to be the 'modest witness' from above, scientific, all-knowing, objective, removed and superior, granting him epistemological and social power (Haraway 1997). Information needs to be safeguarded. It is recognized as powerful, and yet paradoxically, in need of protection. The uncensored free flow of information is dangerous. As a powerful instrument, it is a 'double-edged sword' that can be utilized for positive or destructive purposes because it can be appropriated, damaged, distorted, or exploited by the wrong people. It is this researcher's responsibility then to manage and control the information, deciding who he considers to be eligible to exchange this secret knowledge. That eligibility is based on trust. Trustworthiness is grounded in both knowing how to 'safely manage' the knowledge, and knowing who else can have access. In this sense, information becomes a private and exclusive property. The researcher has established a form of ownership, in effect, creating a new political economy of information capital that is only exchanged with the others he trusts, that is, only with other CARO members. In its political and cultural contexts, CARO's technology-in-practice effectively transfers security and threat solutions to the individual CARO member, thus privatizing and politicizing information exchange.

Therefore, the selection of each individual into CARO is vitally important. In this privatized group of technical experts, each member becomes an important link within the trust network.

RESEARCHER DANIEL: CARO is an organization of top-level experts in the world. There are very few and membership is very restrictive because you have to be, first, a top-level

antivirus researcher. You have to prove you are very knowledgeable. Second, you have to be trustworthy. And third,
you have to be willing to contribute for the benefit of the
group. All of these three factors are equally important. I
mean, no matter how good you are, if you don't have the
time to help the others and be active and come to work,
you aren't going to be elected to CARO. Because of this restrictive membership, very few people can be a member of
CARO. And within CARO we have a mailing list which we
use to send viruses to each other.

CARO's membership is 'very restrictive'. Based on expertise, trust,
and a commitment to help others, election into CARO excludes those
who are not worthy.

As the CARO member above states, there is an expectation of reciprocity with the other members of CARO. CARO members will post
a contribution to a virus threat or malware development in their private e-mail list with the expectation of reciprocal exchange, though not
in a quid pro quo fashion. Information is not traded directly, but is
'gifted' to the group with the expectation that each will use, develop,
and then contribute results back to the group. Exchanging information
interlocks the CARO members into a social framework imbued with a
range of obligations, meanings, and power relationships (Derrida
1997; Mauss 1967).

Community and Power

CARO's exclusive e-mail list demonstrates that knowledge is not neutral but is linked with the operation of power (Foucault 1972). The
CARO members manage the knowledge information system: who is
eligible, its distribution, and its application. Through their exclusive
technical and institutional knowledge about computer viruses, through
their management and 'ownership' of this knowledge, their membership within CARO becomes a form of capital—economic, social, political, and cultural. CARO members become the 'go to' people
requested on government committees and commercial expansion enterprises. As the technical, ethical, and moral leaders of the antivirus
industry, they are the 'tribal elders' and authoritative spokespersons.

One vendor describes these 'senior' researchers' influence over the antivirus industry:

> VENDOR TIMOTHY: In the AV industry, a lot of power is with the individuals, with the people who tell their companies what they should be doing with this whole antivirus thing. And those are the people who, you know, the people like [Researcher Michael], the people like [Researcher Thomas]. Those are the people who can control. Time, you know, pushes one up the chain. These people have the power now to tell their companies what's going to happen. They have much more power than the average techie. They have the power.

The researchers' ability to influence company practice—to 'tell their companies what they should be doing' is recognized as a form of social power. Power is located in the researchers' authority, knowledge, and influence. Much more than the 'average techie', these researchers are seen to directly influence the antivirus vendors' directions and goals. That power is magnified, however, as this localized influence is perceived to radiate out from one company to influencing the antivirus industry as a whole. Indeed, the researchers' influence is articulated as key to how the entire antivirus industry functions. Individually and collectively, the researchers are perceived as the legitimate compass of the antivirus industry, telling these companies 'what they should be doing'. 'They have the power'.

Within this privatized elite structure of information exchange, collaboration is through peer-to-peer networking. The CARO researcher freely contributes to the efforts of other CARO members, forming an epistemological community based on sharing pooled information:

> RESEARCHER WILLIAM: From the outside it is always put on like a sort of conflict, but I don't have any problems talking to any other, any of the competitors, and sharing the information because we all trust each other. Now I can present something which is new in the technical sense, and the next time it is them. Maybe some of the bigger companies have more CARO members working for them and they

may give more. But each time, they also get something
more back. You get much more than doing it yourself. It's
a resource problem.

The shared research done by CARO is not portrayed as a quid pro
quo, but as a collaborative solution to a lack of resources of any one researcher working without the CARO multi-perspective input. The
results of their collective contributions are unmatched by the individualized knowledge of a lone researcher. Their collective knowledge
can also be more quickly applied toward the solution of a global outbreak. Working together generates a more rapid response.

Besides addressing the urgency in a malware attack, CARO members can also 'present something new'. Members generate new projects
on their own initiative, while other members give suggestions and discuss problems arising from their own programming practices. Vendors
that have several CARO members as employees may be able to contribute more to the group. That being the case, all researchers are still
seen as reliant upon the collaborative knowledge. Their individual
research output is still portrayed as somewhat isolated and under-
resourced without the CARO collaboration.

'Outsiders', those not in CARO, are seen as evaluating this kind of
cooperative orientation and priority as a conflict, viewing the sharing
of information from competing antivirus vendors as problematic.
These outsiders, as I did in the beginning, do not detach the researchers from their commitments and loyalties to their employers.
However, CARO members do not view their colleagues through the
competitive lens of profits and products and do not commercially compete against each other over knowledge claims.

In sharp contrast to the world of corporations and government bu-
reaucracies that claim secret and intellectual property rights as the
source of their power and wealth, CARO is portrayed as drawing on
the collaborative internet and academic tradition of sharing discoveries and communicating with peers to improve their collective ideas.
Indeed, many antivirus professionals idealize the CARO researcher as
a kind of antidote to the competitive skirmishes between vendors:

> CORPORATE END USER ANDY: The good side is, when you get
> let in to the 'inner sanctum', if you like, of the researchers,

the technical guys, you do realize that it is a very solid kind of band of brothers. And they don't have anything like the bickering and the backstabbing or anything else that goes on higher up the chain.

Many antivirus professionals commented about how CARO researchers are above the commercialized interests of business and the daily politics of corporate competition. Their collaborative process of innovation and problem solving takes place with open communication free from competitive drivers. These researchers are seen by many within the industry as separate from these everyday politics of the industry, and as collectively more able to find solutions to malicious code attacks because they are not constrained by 'bickering and backstabbing'. They are the 'inner sanctum' of the industry, freed from the continual calculations of corporate sales agendas. They do their collaborative research as if it were a calling, performed as if it were an end unto itself in order to create something socially valuable to protect the networked community. CARO epitomizes the best of the industry.

The Dark Side of Trust: Profiting from Exclusions

This trusting collaborative network has larger social-structural ramifications. For CARO members, trust is grounded in their individualized social interactions. While experienced as an almost blind faith connection between individuals with whom they are willing to exchange information, it also becomes a foundation for other relationships by excluding those with whom they are unwilling to share their secret knowledge. CARO has erected a hierarchical structure through their informal technical group and established a code of right and wrong, good and bad, and definitions of threats and security, trustworthy and untrustworthy, that have real-world implications.

For example, the CARO members' economic value, material wealth, and purchasing power are increased as each vendor vies to hire and keep as many CARO members as they can. Because there are only about twenty-five of these experts in the entire world, they are seen as a vital and limited resource to the development of the industry and are recruited and paid accordingly by their employers.

RESEARCHER WILLIAM: Even though CARO is privately based,
if I switch companies, my company right now does not get
another CARO member in return. I just take my CARO
membership with me. And of course that also is a commercial value for your own.

I: Absolutely, because you can take that information that is
shared to solve a problem and then turn it into a company
profit.

RESEARCHER WILLIAM: Yes. And it's a private market value for
me, so, I mean, you can't sell it. You don't get money on it
in that way. But people do regard it as important.

The power relations inherent with systems of recognition, defer-
ence, and rewards are all observable in the respect and status attributed to the category and social authority of the CARO researcher.
Being part of CARO gives the antivirus researcher social and economic power. CARO's network of trust and their peer-to-peer network
reinforce an established social hierarchy and differential power relationships. Trust as defined by the CARO researchers consequently becomes a form of capital within the antivirus industry, generating forms
of exclusivity that affect access to resources.

Another real-world consequence of the CARO trust-network is the
effect of its exclusivity. The process of reciprocally exchanging secret
and private information reinforces social statuses circulating around
that pooled information.[4] The exchanged information sets a pattern of
inclusion and exclusion that turns people into social categories of insid-
ers and outsiders. The need for exclusivity is promoted as this CARO
member discusses the practice of sharing and exchanging information:

RESEARCHER DANIEL: Viruses, they're dangerous, they're sensitive. Accidents can happen if you send viruses to people

---

[4] This information exchange is a small part of the larger political economy of information. It is similar in many ways to a 'gift economy'. Analysis of 'the gift' has provided
an elaborate framework for understanding cultural economies and especially for understanding the social relationships entailed. Marcel Mauss's (1967) discussions of
reciprocity in gift giving inspired generations of anthropologists, folklorists, and cultural theorists to consider the complexities and significance of gift giving. For

who aren't qualified to handle them or aren't trustworthy to handle them. Just because somebody has an antivirus product does not automatically mean that they are qualified or trustworthy to have the viruses.

Through their exclusivity, CARO attempts to insure against the dangers inherent in sharing viruses and information about viruses. Because viruses are dangerous, a superior level of technical competence is required to 'handle them'. Indeed, CARO selectively decides who is eligible and who is not eligible to receive the secret information. This process defines the boundaries of CARO as a technically privileged group. Those insider–outsider boundaries exclude others as unqualified, including vendors with antivirus products. According to CARO, producing an antivirus product is not a qualification. By stigmatizing and denying others access to their privileged information, their exclusive reciprocal relationships reinforce their high-status position as elite researchers within the knowledge/power techno-meritocracy. Their exclusive reciprocal relationships establish their pooled information as a highly valued and limited product, increasing both their social and financial capital in a continuing reproductive exclusionary cycle.

How each CARO member then applies this highly valued pooled knowledge with his employer is where the impact of this information exchange has larger implications. The 'returns', the knowledge produced from the generosity and the bonds of solidarity within CARO, are funneled into competitive vendor products. Each CARO member applies the knowledge generated from the 'technical group' to his employer's antivirus software. Their shared knowledge is interpreted by each vendor's research and development team into a commodity that can be bought and sold to corporate customers.

RESEARCHER WILLIAM: CARO was started as a group of people officially drinking beer [laughs]. Perhaps we should move up from there. CARO started as a group of friends with

---

elaborations on the social systems of exchange, look at Claude Levi-Strauss's (1987) understanding of reciprocity and exchange as the basis of kinship relationships, and Annette Weiner's (1983) studies of exchange as a foundation for negotiating value and identity.

the same interests. And we share samples and technology. When we have researched something, we make it public knowledge, public in CARO. How people want to use it or implement it or not, that's their own business. But that way we can cope with problems much faster. And we don't have that many experts in the world at the same level that we can do all the work by ourselves all the time, so we help each other out a little bit here and there. Technically we help each other. Commercially we kill each other.

The technical is separated from the commercial. There is a division between his group of friends with the same research interests and their roles as employees of competing vendors. The limited supply of antivirus experts generates a gap in specialist knowledge, creating a need to pool information and to work cooperatively. In CARO, they see each other as friends and colleagues. That perspective, however, is limited to solving malware threats. CARO researchers are employed by, work for, and have loyalties to competing antivirus vendors. This cleavage results in a simultaneous need to cooperate with, and yet compete against, other CARO members. How their pooled knowledge about malware threats is applied in antivirus products is commercial, is constructed separately as the 'implementation' of knowledge. Implementation of knowledge at the business–vendor level is a site of fierce competition.

Begun as a loose, informal organization of drinking buddies, CARO became institutionalized, and as such, crystalized and rigidified its structures. The free exercise of communication dedicated to solving malware threats became hegemonic, cementing the knowledge, the means of production, and the authority of its members. 'Public in CARO' draws upon the concept of open access to knowledge and information in cyberspace, unconfined and unrestricted by corporate borders or limits. 'Public in CARO' connects to the need to cooperatively share essential ideas and solutions, ignoring artificial boundaries established by the competitive market strategies between antivirus vendors. However, 'public in CARO' also restricts the knowledge so it remains within the confines of the CARO trust network. 'Public in CARO' merely reproduces exclusive knowledge and power hierarchies.

In the information society, technology and information are decisive tools in generating profits and appropriate market shares, leading to the interweaving and interdependence of high technology and financial capital. CARO as an organization of elite technological researchers working for competing vendors reflects this technology/information/commerce nexus. Because CARO members are at the borders of the science, technology, academic, and corporate worlds, they have a unique opportunity and advantage of connecting various aspects of diverse information flows. Since their networks are multiple, the knowledge they can draw from is also multiple and interdisciplinary, contributing to the whole more than any one individual could. Indeed, their workplaces at the borders of telecommunications and information-processing industries are transformed into sites of knowledge production, and their contribution to actual antivirus products boosts the power and authority of their scientific expertise. CARO's elite knowledge is established as the highest accomplishment of the industry, a knowledge that is unavailable and unintelligible to the 'untrustworthy' and 'unqualified'. CARO members cultivate their elite status through utilizing and manipulating the information accessed from their multiple networks, and are granted authority and prestige by those who have no such competence or access. In this sense they become a 'knowledge monopoly', having control over the intersections of various technologies and networks. They accumulate power and inevitably form a powerful monopoly against those who are denied access to their specialized knowledge.

Thus there are some obvious tensions surrounding CARO members. The communal cooperative exchange of information grants CARO members both ethical and technological authority as they work to solve malware issues. To prevent threatened, dangerous information escaping from the control of CARO, a trust network is established to thwart attempts to appropriate, damage, or distort that information. In their efforts to establish their authority and ownership over information, in their desire to protect it, and in their need to manipulate and reapply it into competitive software, economic value is also attached to their now secret, private, and sacred information. This process results in the commodification of both their information and their positions as CARO members. CARO is granted both economic and social capital, and the knowledge produced is transformed into a form of information capital.

While CARO members may be significant to the entire antivirus industry, individually they are also critically important to the responsiveness of the specific antivirus vendor that employs them. To have a

CARO researcher as part of an antivirus company can be vital to that company's ability to compete in the marketplace. The cooperation of the 'brotherhood' allows the 'pooled' information to be a resource for the researcher and consequently, information that can be applied to a vendor's product. The CARO researcher becomes a valuable commodity himself, based on this unique access to vital information.

The industry's support of CARO's exclusive membership qualification reproduces and supports the development of these researchers' individual power and their domination as digital elites. As powerful elites, they embed their social values in antivirus products, a process that legitimates these same individuals gaining an even greater ability to act upon and affect the industry. Issues of intentionality and use, as well as infrastructure and access, are controlled by these CARO members. Through their use of exclusivity and secrecy, which have little to do with the technology per se, they have the ability to shape and affect information about, and solutions for, computer viruses.

CARO's knowledge is entwined with the mythical beginnings of the internet, is socially located within both corporate and scientific realms, and is able to continually reestablish its knowledge and power base through maintaining its access to exclusive secret knowledge. Through this position, CARO attempts to dominate the antivirus industry by constraining and managing an exclusive knowledge network.

Vendors

CARO's exclusive network, however, is not a neutral or value-free system, and is challenged by some in the antivirus industry as an unfair and unproductive closed system. The legitimation and institutionalization of CARO's secret, exclusive knowledge is questioned by those who have been excluded from its network of trust. Specifically, most CARO members are employed by antivirus vendors; however, CARO members view vendors as businesses, as an amalgamation of individuals 'outside' the trust network. Vendors, both those with and those without CARO researchers, respond to this struggle, articulating the inconsistencies and real-world consequences of CARO's domination, organizing themselves into an alternative information exchange network. Exchanging information about viruses then becomes a dynamic arena of struggle exposing industry contradictions and contestations.

REVS is an acronym for Rapid Exchange of Virus Samples. It was an organization of antivirus vendors formed by a non-CARO antivirus professional in 1999. Vendors who joined REVS agreed to trust each other, both by exchanging virus samples and by sharing reports on the current attacks infecting their corporate customers, with all other members in the organization. In an emergency outbreak, there is a special need for the rapid exchange of information, a speedy response that CARO's trust network cannot necessarily accommodate. Indeed, many vendors described CARO's emergency response as 'slow and bloated' as researchers huddled together analyzing the virus. Vendors that joined REVS agreed to cooperate and share vital information gathered across their diverse customer networks. Placing protection of the internet as their highest priority, REVS members were willing and able to coordinate among themselves as vendors with a wide and disparate customer base, to be responsive in an emergency, and to react and collaborate as a network and alliance. As non-elites, they formed a powerful medium for communication, supporting each other's struggles and creating the equivalent of an alternative network, a new insider group.

REVS challenged the individualization of CARO's exclusive network, and established a new additional information exchange network directly between antivirus companies. The membership criteria of REVS was the significant point. While CARO's membership was individually-based, REVS's information exchange was vendor-based. Antivirus companies joined REVS, not specific antivirus professionals. In an emergency virus outbreak, vendors who had joined REVS would be able to exchange information about viruses, including 'live' virus samples. REVS's membership was seen to reflect the actual organizational structure of the industry.

VENDOR TIMOTHY: Companies are the ones that are doing this. Companies are the ones that, when I want to buy a piece of antivirus software, I don't go to [Researcher Michael] or [Researcher Keith] and say, "I want to buy a piece of antivirus software, please sell me one." You go to [Antivirus Vendor], or [Antivirus Vendor], or [Antivirus Vendor], or whatever it is and you say, "I want to buy a piece of antivirus software for my million-people company, please help me out here." And so why is it, that it is *people* that control the whole virus thing? Why is it that we distribute viruses between people and we claim that it's not? Because people work for certain companies? Is it because they are 'good guys' and they know what they're doing? I don't find that very satisfying. It seems to me that it is the companies that should be the ones that are, what's the word I want here, in the 'loop'.

This vendor is aware of the real-world repercussions of abruptly being out of the individualized CARO information 'loop', having experienced the sudden, unexpected, and extended loss of its one and only CARO member. Working around the extended loss crystalized for him the limited contributions of CARO knowledge to virus management at the corporate site, the unnecessary constraints around CARO's secret information exchange, and the circumscribed role CARO members play as vendor employees. He suggests that the information processing, the development of antivirus software, and the interactions between buyers and vendors is in reality, a vendor-to-corporate customer process, not an individualized transaction with a CARO member. According to this vendor, antivirus vendors are the 'real' information exchange units.

The struggle over information exchange about computer viruses demarcates a digital divide, a division induced by unequal access to CARO's secret information. Some vendors organized REVS as an attempt to counter CARO individuals as the informational 'haves', and the rest of the industry as the 'have nots', a divide that is highlighted during an outbreak. CARO's hierarchy marginalized vendors as 'outsiders', as an intermingling of the unqualified, the untrustworthy, an 'underclass'. As an underclass, vendors are barred from this exchange of information and then must negotiate with the CARO members over resources and access. Being kept 'out of the loop' is tantamount to being socially, economically, and politically marginalized. Even though antivirus professionals working for vendors are computer literate and savvy, even though they have access to corporate buyers and the financial capital to develop software, they are still indebted to and depend upon the CARO elites' monopolized communication of information.

REVS then established an information exchange network between vendors as alternative units of potential knowledge. As the companies actually developing antivirus software, as the endpoint receiving reports from their customers about outbreaks, they could share ideas, virus samples, and relevant strategies. In this way, vendors rejected being just passive pawns controlled by the CARO interpretation of the technological environments. Through information exchange between antivirus vendors, the vendors became an amalgamated group of antivirus professionals and active players in the industry. Penetrating and contesting CARO's stigmas, they responded strategically and innovatively to the pressures of being left out of the loop. REVS challenged the institutionalization of CARO's hierarchical knowledge structure, generating a struggle over the circulation of CARO's proprietary information.

Symbolic Annihilations

Most CARO members rejected REVS as a viable alternative exchange network. The CARO member below maintains his responsibility to be a gatekeeper of the entire industry. He negates the very organizational structure of REVS and its claim as an alternative and reliable strategic alliance:

> RESEARCHER DANIEL: My problem with REVS is the people, is that the implementation of this otherwise good idea, is very bad. One fundamental problem is that membership in REVS is corporate-based. That is, a company is a member, and when you send a virus to the list, all you know is that people from that company will receive it. You don't know who. What if the marketing department gets it? When I am sending a virus, I want to know who receives it. I want to know who has the responsibility for it. I want to know if that company leaks it, who to blame. I can't blame the company in general. I must know I gave the virus to you, and it is your responsibility because it leaked.

This CARO member recognizes that there is a need for an alternative to the slow CARO communication network. Indeed, REVS is a 'good idea'. It had just been 'implemented badly'. While praising the idea, he undermines the competencies of REVS by identifying the inability of vendors to control information, to know who is personally responsible, and who can be blamed and held accountable should information escape. Stating three times that 'I want to know', 'I want to know', 'I want to know', he strongly negates REVS's corporate-based model of information exchange, highlighting his authority and legitimacy as part of the knowledge monopoly of CARO. Emphasizing the need for information to be contained within an individualized exclusive communication system, CARO's privatized and secret knowledge practice is the unspoken exemplar, upheld as the model for personal responsibility, a community of competence and skillful practice that can securely exchange dangerous information. CARO sees itself as a safeguard against the fast-paced transformations of technology and the growth of antivirus vendors as an amalgamation of ever-changing, multivocational employees. CARO is the stable connection in an unstable environment.

This CARO member also focuses on the inability to trust vendors and their marketing departments. Several antivirus vendor marketing departments are known to have given 'live' infectious virus samples to potential customers as a public relations' promotional strategy to demonstrate their product's competitive edge. The public relations' strategy allowed the customer to be part of the vendor's inner circle by testing the vendor's software on the 'live' virus sample. This type of public relations is negated as reckless and irresponsible. It is considered 'absurd' and 'idiotic' to put live viruses in the hands of 'unprofessionals' and 'naïve' users. As a marketing technique, it breaches the security and boundaries of the trust network, compounding the problems of an already insecure internet. Being seen as having no technological benefit, the vendor marketing strategy is labeled merely 'opportunistic'.

Vendors, with their opportunistic marketing departments and multi-vocational professionals, are therefore, outside the trust network. According to CARO's standards, REVS has no effective control parameters for containing and securing virus samples. Vendors are 'commerce', and when commerce becomes involved in the exchange of secret information, the information is no longer protected. With REVS, virus samples become a potential marketing ploy where ultimate control is lost. The same CARO member continues:

RESEARCHER DANIEL: So, in such cases it is very difficult to establish trust on a company basis. I mean let's take a company like [Antivirus Vendor]. There are at [Antivirus Vendor] members of CARO, which means that I trust them implicitly. I send them viruses every day. But, I will never say that I trust the company [Antivirus Vendor], especially because of what they have done in the past. I will never send a virus just to the company. No way. You establish trust between people, people who you know, you have had reason to expect that they will behave properly. You can't trust a company. That's at least one fundamental problem.

REVS is negated because, as an organization of vendors, it cannot know or control its members' employees. The CARO member again asserts that knowledge of and trust in people is the only legitimate basis for competent and secure information exchange relationships. Profit motives and the transience and anonymity of the vendors' workforce prevent the application of CARO's security model. CARO's trust network can only be reproduced through the self-enforcing discipline of known and trusted individuals.

His emphasis on 'knowing' individuals also reveals a concern about the anonymity inherent within internet technology. Conflating trust and control, an antivirus company becomes an unmanageable complexity, an unknown, unsanctionable assemblage of non-CARO members who could freely and anonymously use the internet to exchange viruses. Trust in this sense becomes the ability to predict the behaviors of others, the fulfilment of expectations for proper actions, and a mode of surveillance and control over the like-minded and known. If the individual is unknown, if the person or persons are anonymous, they are seen as uncontrollable. Vendors are untrustworthy. Their lack of ability to securely handle dangerous information is unacceptable. He continues:

RESEARCHER DANIEL: The second fundamental problem is that the sender has no control on who will receive the virus we send. If you send the virus, anybody, any of the members will receive it. Now imagine that some problem has occurred, for instance [Antivirus Vendor], who has a member, has behaved unethically. I now have a problem with that. And I don't want to send him the virus. With the structure of

REVS, the only choice you get is not to send the virus to
anybody. Then there are also minor problems like, as I have
explained to you already, I don't like the word 'exchange'.
But they have put that in their name. But those are minor
things and they can be fixed. But, for instance, such things
like membership have to be individual, not company-based.
This is very important, and they have blatantly refused to
change that.

This CARO member does not believe in vendors' goodwill, reliability, or competence, as demonstrated by REVS's 'blatant' refusal to
accommodate CARO suggestions. This CARO member does not trust
the organized irresponsibility inherent in corporate businesses that allows amorphous and fluid individuals to deny accountability. 'Anybody'
in the company can receive the potentially destructive information. If
a person has behaved 'unethically', this CARO member wants the option of not sending the virus to him specifically, simultaneously protecting the net from his future unethical behaviors, and punishing his
action by excluding him from the information flow.

Punishment by CARO is implemented through technological exclusion. By preventing a vendor or individual from receiving virus
samples, by keeping them out of the loop, the vendor and individual
are unable to generate a prompt viable solution to a threat. Vendors
are practical commercial entities having millions of dollars riding on
their specific antivirus architecture. They compete over the quickest
response times, measuring the minutes from virus release to vendor
software updates, ranking each other's attempts to protect corporate
network flows. Without the virus sample, this unethical person or the
unethical vendor becomes isolated and unproductive.

Consequently, CARO members use exclusion as a form of punishment to keep vendors and their marketing departments in line. By potentially penalizing them through the real threat of exclusion, CARO
in fact utilizes exclusion as a disciplinary technique. The more money
there is at stake, the less inclined vendors are to bear the costs of isolation from the CARO knowledge monopoly. Since vendors' economic
considerations are seen to outweigh the ethics and security of the internet, CARO usurps and redirects the vendor's financial priorities by
enforcing conformity to its security ideals and criteria.

Objections to REVS moved from theoretical debates about security and trust to threats of exclusion. CARO's negation of REVS became a deployment of moralizing discourses about security, strategies of corporate capitalism, and assurances of exclusion. CARO, acting as the self-promoted industry regulator, assumed it had the exclusive right to judge and evaluate organizational ethics and technological applications. Subverting REVS's representation as an equal partner in the fight to save the internet, CARO singled out REVS as threatening to undermine the technological security of the entire internet.

To address the challenges raised by REVS, several CARO members created an alternative networked organization. It is called the Anti-Virus Emergency Discussion group, or AVED. The CARO member from above continues his discussion:

> RESEARCHER DANIEL: We had a meeting within CARO and my position was that I would really rather that we convince them to fix the thing. Because we have other work to do. I mean, I am really disappointed that every time somebody outside CARO decides to do something serious in the antivirus field, they screw up like they did this time. It's not that difficult to do. But obviously they are not going to change. And that's why some of us within CARO, but it's not a CARO initiative, have started this parallel organization, AVED, which is supposed to perform the same kind of service based on the same idea, except that it implements it properly.

After all the debate, CARO members acknowledge that REVS members are 'not going to change'. In response, CARO organizes another 'parallel organization' to address the 'screw ups' of REVS, which was initially envisioned by vendors to address the shortcomings of CARO. By offering this alternative to REVS and by addressing vendors' concerns about CARO's slow rate of response, AVED is put forth as the legitimate secure alternative.

With AVED, the system of obligations, responsibilities, and mutuality is supposedly clear, visible, and knowable. With AVED, viruses are not sent to 'just anybody', but to 'people you know'. Implemented 'properly', the AVED system is oppositionally framed as transparent and accountable. CARO in effect has actively determined what can be documented as a threat, what will be addressed, what is visible and of concern, and its importance. According to CARO, trusting the CARO–AVED approach reduces the complexity of the unknown and the uncontrollable with the expectation that viruses will remain contained and safe within the borders defined by CARO members.

REVS's concerns, the motivation driving its organization, ultimately lost support. REVS was symbolically annihilated. Threatened with exclusion from network flows, and offered as a sanctioned alternative to CARO's slow and bloated crisis responses, antivirus professionals rejected REVS and joined AVED. A few weeks after the preceding interviews ended, REVS no longer existed as an organization. A CARO researcher discusses CARO as a 'power block' that terminated REVS:

> RESEARCHER KEITH: The difference, the fundamental difference between AVED and REVS, is that AVED was regrettably implemented because the people who were strongly, strongly against the REVS model of trusting companies didn't manage to convince the people who were running REVS to change that fundamental core of how it worked.
> I: Isn't that one of the basic problems and basic issues though? REVS wanted to be company-based and not individually-based?
> RESEARCHER KEITH: Well it depends. See, you've framed that, you said it was a problem. I don't think it is a problem. It is a problem for a small to moderate number of powerful, significant, top of the . . . the sort of the generally respected group of antivirus researchers. And those people form a fairly significant power block. And so if you do something that they're not happy with that affects or reflects on the industry as a whole, they are quite likely to try to do something about it, for better or worse.

Symbolic struggles such as the REVS–AVED controversy pit those in subordinate positions against those in superordinate positions. CARO understands itself and is recognized by antivirus professionals as a 'power block'. The struggle places those with a monopoly over the definition and distribution of information against those who attempt to usurp those advantages. REVS critiqued CARO's privatized knowledge and generation of an exclusive technical expertise and hierarchy. CARO relegates vendors to an underclass on the grounds that they just don't know enough, they have 'screwed up' again.

CARO's strategy to isolate REVS promoted its own identity and power. CARO members reasserted their identity as the legitimate judges of the antivirus industry, and REVS as the 'idiots' unable to implement proper procedures. CARO is renowned as the epitome of technical expertise and ethics. Consequently, the interpretation of the antivirus industry's 'needs' and 'interests' are considered primarily through CARO's dominant authority and perspective. This strategy becomes a self-fulfilling prophecy as the vendors are kept out of the loop, turning low vendor knowledge into a stigmatized attribute. By creating a culture of secrecy, information is kept as the private and exclusive property of CARO, and vendors remain merely the sellers and marketers of the end product.

Negation of Researchers as Experts

Total control and complete domination, however, are never realizable. Within the fast-paced technical evolution of antivirus software, legitimating the dominant definition of what is and who are 'acceptable' is a constant process of negotiation. Thus, while REVS may have died a symbolic death, other forms of resistance to CARO remain. And while the power balance may not seem to have shifted, and the CARO-supported AVED model is now the viable emergency response system, many of the REVS assumptions and foundational critiques are still in circulation. While many of those interviewed conceptualized CARO as significant and important, others increasingly suggested that CARO has outlived its usefulness. For many, CARO is seen to have created a power relationship that no longer serves the industry and is preventing the industry from evolving.

> VENDOR MARK: Well, I think that the old guard, if you want to define it like that, have been pedaling for far too long the nonsense that virus research is some sort of God-given right and God-given gift, and that only themselves can do

it properly. It has been shown that you can train antivirus researchers and that's precisely what everybody's doing.

I: Great. So you see a new crop of researchers coming out?

VENDOR MARK: Well, certainly if you look around our labs, you don't have many you might consider of the old guard. We have youngsters who have been trained in the art and trained very well. It just takes some time. It just takes some time to train people.

This vendor suggests that the entire antivirus industry has changed. The 'old guard' and their 'God-given rights' are succeeded by well-trained 'youngsters'. The exclusive network of the CARO trust model is made redundant through education and a type of apprenticeship. Others suggest that CARO is 'bloated' and self-serving, limiting the evolution of the industry. Some mock CARO's symbolic authority and prestige.

CORPORATE END USER ALEX: I mean I slightly feel that CARO is being used as a, you know, they say, "Look you must be great. You must be wonderful. We respect you so much, you are in CARO." Whereas actually CARO is fairly point-less and futile. It's like you get, you know, it's like you are being offered a knighthood in England just for being a pop singer or something [laughs]. Like Cliff Richard or some-one. He's now Sir Cliff Richard. Big bloody deal. But I do think they think, "Oooh, I'm in CARO, so I am untouch-able." It's bollocks [nonsense] you know.

CARO's motivation is also critiqued. CARO researchers are no longer seen as the epitome of ethical behavior, but are also motivated by financial concerns:

VENDOR TIMOTHY: It's an awful incredible amount of power in the hands of the CARO members, because they suddenly become immensely marketable because the companies want these viruses. They have to have these viruses. And the only way they can get them is through the CARO member. So the CARO members have done pretty well out of this, which is fine. They probably didn't do it deliberately. But they're certainly aware of the side effect.

And CARO's ability to maintain its own ideals, goals, and power are questioned by some of the CARO members themselves. As the CARO researchers move up the corporate ladder and out of antivirus research, their membership affiliations are questioned:

> RESEARCHER KEITH: Well, you see that is a bit of a thorny issue. What do you do with these people who have only relatively peripheral links with the antivirus industry anymore? But when you set the organization up, or in the first five years of the organization or whatever, were actually really significant, they were primary product developers of significant products. What do you do with those people?

CARO seems to have stagnated, unable to effectively adapt to the constantly evolving networks of information alliances. CARO membership has remained stable over the past ten years, with few additions or resignations while the industry itself has gone through major transformations. And my interviews highlight how CARO's notoriety is contained within the small world of the antivirus industry. Those who work in internet security and apply antivirus technology at corporate sites, but are not subscribers to *Virus Bulletin*, nor attendees at antivirus conferences, had never heard of CARO.

On all its pillars of symbolic authority, CARO is challenged. From their God-like, rock-star status, they are critiqued for being 'in' the world. They are seen to be aware of their elitism, and yet they hold back the entire industry with their outmoded and outdated zealous exclusivity. The repercussions of their agendas are seen as having a stranglehold on the industry, a hold that is slowly being replaced by well-educated 'youngsters'. The substance of the mutual reciprocal relations of trust is challenged as peripheral, as outmoded, as contaminated by financial concerns. CARO's domination of the antivirus industry is thus not total. Even though REVS is no longer in existence, it is evidence of one of many of the resistant critiques questioning the basis of power and authority inherent in CARO's exclusivity.

Antivirus Researchers, Power, and Technology

There are always struggles over the very definitions and meanings of the most valued resources. This is particularly true where knowledge rapidly changes. Because the antivirus industry is by definition dynamic, its forms of authority are constantly negotiated by its players, which in a reciprocal fashion, transform the nature of the industry.

CARO determined the industry concepts through which the internet was understood as continually threatened by unknown and untrustworthy others. Yet this knowledge frame is not taken for granted by vendors, whose daily real-world practices challenge these exclusive experts' claims. REVS's background and technology-in-practice resulted from different assumptions and perspectives of the best way to deal with an outbreak. REVS framed the problems of exchanging 'emergency' virus samples and information to be an issue of access, not trust. According to REVS, the CARO expert was far removed from the daily, real-world effects and the urgency of meeting customer demands.

According to CARO, however, REVS's vendors were commercial entities. They were a high-risk social group operating on the borders of capitalist enterprises and virus protection. When commerce is invested in computer viruses, CARO feared that those commercial entities would potentially control the viruses. CARO constructed vendors as 'other', as potentially unscrupulous and unethical, requiring control and containment. In CARO's view, REVS became part of the virus problem instead of part of the antivirus solution.

The divergence between CARO's and REVS's understandings of threat, trust, and security reveals how membership within different groups within the same industry affects perceptions of 'the problem'. Threat and security knowledges are historical and local, grounded in the daily experiences of each of these groups. What is perceived to be 'risky' for CARO was not experienced as such by REVS vendors in their daily interactions. As a result, their differing security knowledges were contested and subject to disputes and debates over their nature, their control, and who was to blame for their creation.

CARO successfully eliminated REVS because it effectively injected a counter logic that reconstructed vendors as unreliable and unstable.

CARO was portrayed as the center of expertise, security, and reliability, insisting the industry adopt its interpretations of formal and procedural solutions. CARO had the power to reproduce its vision of the industry through excluding the noncompliant from the necessary information, while offering an alternative networked flow. CARO members symbolically annihilated REVS by refusing to include REVS members within their information exchange. Other vendors and other corporations could not afford to be out of the protection of the cabal. REVS as an organization only lasted about a year and was replaced by AVED, another networked response list that is more inclusive and open than CARO, but is still based on knowledge of, and trust in, individuals.

The long-term effects, however, took their toll on CARO's prestige and status as 'the' moral and technical foundation of the antivirus industry. Through their need to eliminate REVS, they had to articulate their moral and technical credentials and objectives, drawing attention to themselves for review by the rest of the industry. Through this and other confrontational processes, the inconsistencies and conflicts of their 'mission' were scrutinized and found by many to be lacking. As the top of the techno-meritocracy of the antivirus industry, as the moral leaders of the industry, CARO members refused to share information, punished the noncompliant, and extracted higher salaries because of their exclusivity. Between the rapid change in technology and the innovations within the antivirus industry, many came to see CARO as the old guard from a cottage industry, technically and ethically irrelevant to current and future social and technological transformations. The struggle for legitimation continues as networked information flows are continually transformed by technological innovations and endangered by the portentous threat of the virus writer.

4 IT Corporate Customers as End Users

Corporate End Users

There are different perspectives and objectives in the antivirus (AV) industry among those who research the solution to protecting technology, those who actually develop and sell antivirus software, and those who purchase and use it. These industry segments variously conceal and share institutional and cultural knowledge systems. Researchers, vendors, and corporate end users continually negotiate over who and what is considered a security threat, and who and what can be trusted with secret information. As we saw in Chapter 3, CARO members see vendors as transient and untrustworthy, needing discipline and surveillance by CARO practices. This chapter is about how vendors project a similar hierarchy on to their corporate end users. While vendors are positioned by CARO as a sort of technological underclass and stigmatized as untrustworthy and unreliable, many vendors regard their corporate end users as ignorant and inept. Through the prism of technological expertise, the corporate end user is constructed as technologically lacking and deficient.

VENDOR TIMOTHY: I am continually amazed when I come to these conferences at the questions that some of the

corporate people ask. The questions display a very deep
failure to understand how, not just viruses, but how viruses
and software, and computers actually work. And that's okay
because they shouldn't have to worry about these things.
But also they should respect, in some senses respect, they
should appreciate the fact that they don't know about
these things, but we do know about at least some of them.
And if we haven't done this thing that they're suggesting,
and we don't want to do it, then that's probably not just because we're selfish and we don't like new things, but probably because it's not a good idea. It sounds all terribly
arrogant, but it. . . . I can't think of a specific example from
this conference, although there have been several instances of customers asking the most amazingly basic questions that reveal fundamental misunderstandings about
how the whole thing works.

This vendor suggests that the 'corporate people' have an inadequate
basic comprehension of computer viruses, demonstrated by them asking
questions that 'reveal fundamental misunderstandings'. Even though he
recognizes they 'should not have to worry' about this knowledge, he ad-
monishes them for their ignorant and unwarranted requests. Instead, he
suggests these ill-equipped corporate people, because of their ignorance, should privilege the vendors' technical expertise and both respect
and appreciate their decisions about product development.

Within the antivirus industry, technical knowledge is privileged
and grants power. The vendors reproduce this hierarchical knowledge
system through elevating both their own and their researchers' technical expertise over corporate end users. Through the determining
prism of the hierarchy of a technological knowledge system, corporate
end users lack authority and are faulted for computer security
breaches. As the system administrators, they are ultimately held responsible for threats against their sites. In discussing 'corporate people', researchers and vendors speak with one voice, one position. Both
conceptualize corporate end users as deficient.

RESEARCHER KEITH: The administrators should be setting up
their systems so that their users can't. . . . The administra-

tors might bemoan that despite the fact that we have told all the staff they are never to do X, Y, and Z, they all, you know, twenty percent of them always do. Well, "duh!" If you are going to keep saying this is the plan, and you know it is going to fail twenty percent of the time, get a better plan! So the responsibility actually is the system administrators. Unfortunately, they are desperately overworked. Most of them are poorly or completely untrained. They are just the people who happened to know most about computers or who were most interested at the time, what I refer to in other contexts as "Bob or Jane from accounts." They are the person who knew the most about PCs in their department or their company or their branch or whatever it might be. And so at some point in history they were given responsibility for looking after the computers.

'Bob and Jane from accounts' are now IT administrators and managers. They are overworked and either poorly or incompletely trained. They are, however, totally responsible for their corporate IT structures. As the corporate end users, they are portrayed as not having the knowledge or disciplinary control over their corporate infrastructure. They lack the 'big picture' of how the technology and corporate sites are entwined and are networked. Instead of accommodating their own staff, 'Bob and Jane from accounts' should be listening to and following researchers' and vendors' directives and 'get a better plan'. Technologically and administratively inadequate, they are on the bottom rung of the antivirus industry's professional security knowledge structure.

Significantly, many corporate end users also acknowledge their lack of technological knowledge. They recognize their dependency on the antivirus industry's technological knowledge systems and its ability to protect their corporate sites. When prioritizing the security of their company assets, corporate end users in charge of their technological infrastructure must rely on their antivirus vendors for protection and technical support. Describing corporate end users as antivirus 'customers', this corporate end user discusses the relationship between customers and their antivirus vendors:

CORPORATE END USER KEVIN: Customers tend to be pretty polite because they are very dependent on the vendors to
help them solve this malware problem.

I: But isn't that a different relationship than most vendors to
customers?

CORPORATE END USER KEVIN: Oh yes, it is. I think the main reason is that technologically most companies aren't equipped
to deal with the malware on their own. So they turn to their
vendors to provide them with tools and the tools have to be
updated constantly. You know, we went from quarterly updates, to monthly updates, to daily updates, to hourly updates when there is a really fast-breaking piece of junk out
there. And, this is what is going on, is corporate customers
can't do it on their own. They know that. So there is a bit of
a dependency on vendors and some vendors exploit that,
unfortunately.

Corporate end users are portrayed as vulnerable, as polite, and as
in need of help and support, because they lack expertise and feel dependent on the antivirus vendor for computer security. They live under the constant threat of an attack, knowing they 'can't do it on their
own'. They are seen, and see themselves, as engulfed by the security
threats to their systems, and as reliant upon their vendors for protection.

Under this logic, the corporate end user is blamed for the disper-
sion of virus outbreaks, for not securing their corporate sites adequately. Taking on board this dominant authoritative interpretation,
the corporate end users are polite in asking for any type of antivirus
technological innovation. However, these requests, as documented in
the previous vendor quote, are interpreted as showing a lack of respect
or appreciation and reveal again the corporate end users' ignorance.
Antivirus vendors are seemingly removed from responsibility for the
corporate end users' computer security and virus problems. The corporate end user is the problem, for being technologically deficient and
for improperly administering his site.

Corporate End Users as Customers

The vendor, researcher, and the corporate end user above conflated the categories of 'corporate people', 'IT administrators', and 'corporate customers'. The blurring of these categories is consistent within the antivirus industry, and as articulated above, they are used interchangeably.[1] The IT manager or administrator, the corporate customer, and the corporate end user coalesce into one technologically deficient stereotype. They lack knowledge, technological insight, and are administratively inadequate. The corporate customer role is also negated with the additional characteristic of being dependent on and exploited by their vendors. As customers, they are invalidated as technologically passive and ignorant.

Knowing their technological deficiencies and paying for protection via their vendors, corporate end users continually and politely request both more information from their vendors, and more opportunities to give relevant feedback to their vendors. Corporate end users repeatedly requested the ability to discuss technological strategies with antivirus vendors, as 'the' knowledge and technology developers, in order to more effectively prepare and protect their corporate technological infrastructure from the continually evolving threats.

> CORPORATE END USER EARL: The thing the vendors are doing right is that they are researching the future. They are coming up with products which meet most of our needs, that meet our requirements. What they're doing wrong is that they are not talking to us early enough and finding out exactly what our problems are. We have to push ourselves forward to get that. And the second thing is, they don't tell us what they're doing. Because I work for a large corporation, I can perhaps get the answers I want. But quite often you will find that they are working on something which has a direct bearing on your strategy, but you don't know that they're doing it. And one of the interesting things about the security arena is that you may think you know all of

---

[1] Following the antivirus industry's usage, for simplicity I, too, conflate this category of corporate administrator and customer/end user into one label of 'corporate end user'.

what the products are going on in your own organization, and then you get a phone call which will totally go off on a tangent. And an AV solution that you rejected just now, may just about be right then. And now you would want that one, but you don't know about it because they didn't tell you about it.

These corporate end users continually strive to maintain a secure computer infrastructure vital to the protection of their companies' communications and products. Rapid changes within their own industries have ripple effects on their needs for computer security and their need for antivirus support. However, corporate end users suggest that vendors do not know, do not understand, and are not interested in the problems at the corporate sites. The corporate end users must 'push ourselves forward' to inform the antivirus industry of their problems, to 'get the answers'. However, as a previous vendor articulated, this 'pushiness' is seen as demonstrating the end user's lack of appreciation and respect for vendors' security knowledge. Product development within the antivirus industry is an obvious site of contestation, as corporate end users suggest, while vendors ignore and negate 'the corporates' perspectives and experiences.

In spite of the vendors' negations, the corporate end users do have unique technological knowledges and valuable experience about their specific sites. From the end user's perspective, the struggle to defend their corporation's technological infrastructure does not mean they lack general technical knowledge skills. Indeed, they see themselves as very adept at maintaining their chosen technologies. The struggle is with the need to outsource and adapt the antivirus security programs to their corporate infrastructure. While vendors are busy developing antivirus software, the actual application, implementation, and the success and failure of these technologies take place at the corporate sites, under control of the corporate end user. The 'real-world' applications of antivirus software entail corporate end users actively engaging with and frequently working around vendors' products.[2] Indeed, corporate end users criticize vendors for developing antivirus products

---

[2] For information on work-arounds, see Ciborra 2002; Button and Sharrock 1998; Suchman 1994; Orlikowski 2000; Pollock 2005.

that are difficult to implement, and for not acknowledging the significance of their role as end users. Corporate end users, 'Bob and Jane from accounts', are the people in charge of and responsible for generating the information necessary for the antivirus industry's actual products and innovative strategies. They are not merely the passive receivers of paid-for protection:

> CORPORATE END USER KEVIN: The vendors think, "We know better. Therefore, you don't know." I mean, there are people who say ninety percent of users are idiots, right? However, the reality of the world is that most of these idiots are the ones giving you your samples, which your product is then based on. And they're the ones who are implementing your new products, which are poorly documented, poorly engineered at times, you know, obscurely configured from the factory, you know. Where is the real problem?

While not denying their technical dependency upon antivirus vendors to battle computer viruses, corporate end users also contest the omission of their contributions. They critique the vendor's assumed all-knowing position within the technological hierarchy. As the corporate end users who carry out the daily tasks of protecting their corporation's assets and technological infrastructures, they call into question their low-level position within the antivirus technology hierarchy, challenging vendors' expertise and power relationships. The corporate end users portray themselves as the labor force of the antivirus industry, as the ones implementing and field-testing antivirus industry products. They are the ones sending samples of viruses to vendors, upon which the vendors' products are based. The corporate end users possess skills and knowledge they see taken for granted by the vendors. Through their daily technology-as-practice, through their work-arounds and creative implementations that interpret confusing software and documentation, corporate end users resist the conceptualization of 'Bob and Jane' as inept and ineffective (Pollock 2005).

It is significant that the corporate end users' technology-in-practice and work-arounds are in some ways expected by the vendors. Corporate end users must necessarily tailor software to their specific corporate site, to massage the antivirus software to work within the corporation's existing software platforms. In this sense, the vendors work with and 'bet on' the skills of their corporate end users to adapt such modifications (Pollock 2005; Latour 1999). Antivirus software is then contingent on and constituted by this ambivalent situation where adaptations are both problematized and expected. This ambivalence in the production of technological knowledge has tended to elide the corporate end user's contribution, resulting in the disqualification and invisibility of 'Bob's and Jane's' skills and knowledges.

The relationships between vendors and the corporate end users are thus continually contested, each operating with different perspectives of their contributions and requirements. From the 'corporate people's' orientation, they must work within vendors' negation for being technologically inept and ignorant, asking for the impossible, not appreciating or respecting vendors' solutions. Within this negative framework, corporate end users learn to negotiate to get their needs meet. A corporate end user from a large multinational corporation states:

> CORPORATE END USER EARL: As a customer of any software vendor, they never meet your needs. Basically, it's a compromise. And because we're a large corporation, we can perhaps put more weight into our case, get changes made. But it's always after the event. But certainly we have had some major successes in influencing vendors in producing things, because we're a big customer. But it's always after the event. It's a two-way process because whenever I talk to a vendor, when I want to put forward some perhaps new ideas on where I see the technology going, I always preface it by saying, "Have you heard this from anybody else?" Because it may be that we're the only one that's had a stab, and that's useful feedback. So we get feedback from them. But they are saying, "Well, you're the only people who are asking for that." And so you go back and rethink it. Yes, still we think we want that. But it gives us an opportunity to take another look at it.

Being a large antivirus customer, this corporate end user seems to have some sway with his vendor. He successfully negotiates getting some of his needs met. He recognizes the need to both confront vendors and rethink his position, developing strategies that allow him to get feedback on his and both other industries' and other corporations' problems.

This negotiation process is structured by and through the commercialization of the antivirus product, and all participants seem to understand this orientation. The commercial orientation grounds this corporate end user's understanding of both his position and the needs of his vendor. Indeed, this corporate IT manager can take the role of his vendor and articulate that position. As a corporate end user, he realizes that his corporation is large and has more weight to 'get changes made'. He has developed strategies, putting forward innovative ideas on where he projects 'the technology is going', and ways of asking polite questions based on his real-world experiences. Because he is a 'big customer', because he understands that he cannot be the 'only people who were asking for that', he also realizes that he may have to 'rethink' his needs. He states that it is a 'two way process', a 'compromise'.

Big customers do have power. Within the market economy, big customers have the ability to 'sway' vendors. The corporate end user above mentions twice that he is a 'large corporation' and a 'big customer'. As 'customers', they have some sovereignty and the ability to force 'compromises'. A vendor explains how antivirus customers have an influence on the industry:

I: You mentioned that customers dictate. Can you explain how they dictate?

VENDOR BRIAN: With their dollars. Our customers tell us, in no uncertain terms, and in certain terms, very, very clearly what they want. You know, my main contingent is the corporate customers, and they tell us what they want. They tell us they want good management. They want good reporting. They want methods of discovery. They want a single management point, you know. They basically tell us how they want to run this software. And if they can't run the software that way, they go to a competitor.

I: Okay, can they dictate technology?

VENDOR BRIAN: No, they can't dictate technology. The only thing they can say is "I want," "I want software to be fastest," or "I don't want software to be the fastest." I mean it really depends. So you have to be flexible enough really. They're not specialists. I mean it's a highly specialized field. But, we cannot dictate to the customers how we want them to operate at their end. I mean, it has got to be solved both ways.

Here corporate end users feature first as self-sufficient and independent consumers, knowledgeable decision makers and arbiters of products. In this conception, consumption of antivirus products is made by well-informed, experienced customers who are conversant and familiar with the requirements and demands of their sites. They have power over vendors by exercising their choice between antivirus competitors. They effectively communicate their wants and needs, always potentially changing to a competitor for better software applications. In this sense, market competition between vendors is seen as a positive, almost democratic form of approval of a vendor's services as the corporate customer 'votes' with his choice of particular antivirus products. Supported by the market logic founded on 'the right to choose', antivirus consumers are seen as dictating production, fueling innovation, and steering 'how the software is run'. The corporate end user as antivirus customer is sovereign, deciding the fate of technical products and ultimately, vendors.

In the next breath however, the vendor above confirms again the exclusive technological hierarchy. These 'choice makers' are not technological experts or specialists. As consumers they can only request— "I want" or "I don't want." They can ask for the fastest update protocol or prioritize other variables over speed. As technological nonspecialists, corporate end users cannot dictate the technology, so the only role left is that of the customer who can request a feature, then react with a yes or no 'vote'. While their inconsistent and unpredictable desires are interpreted as keeping vendors 'flexible', as consumers they are constructed as merely reactive. As such they should respect, appreciate, and accept the vendor's perspective.

Yet the vendor also states, "it has got to be solved both ways," suggesting a mutually interactive process. This equitable distribution scenario suggests a blurred distinction between the users and producers of antivirus innovations. According to the vendors, the continual transformation of antivirus technology incorporates the end users' needs.

Modifications of antivirus products are made on the requests and choices of corporate customers. According to the vendors, they and their corporate customers come to rely on each other as integral parts of the innovative processes, and as mutual resources for the resolution of technical difficulties and problems. The corporate user's decision to stay with an antivirus vendor is interpreted as the measure of the vendor's commercial success.

The emphasis on this two-way process is seen by vendors as a significant contribution to product development.

> VENDOR MARK: It's an iterative process. Nobody can, in my experience, start and say an ideal product will look exactly like this. It's an iterative process with a lot of feedback loops. And it involves prototyping. It involves sales. It involves customer interaction, customer feedback. It involves customers using the product. And the whole thing then starts to evolve.

This continual feedback process supposedly eliminates oppositional requirements and expectations between vendors and their corporate end users as they continually communicate about problems and solutions. Vendors see their corporate customers as linked to them through their mutual needs and technological demands, endlessly informing each other, communicating directly back and forth with the customers in order to ultimately protect corporate sites. The relationship between vendors and their customers is seen as open and flexible, directly reflecting the corporate end user's needs. Vendors see this type of relationship as productive and profitable:

> VENDOR GARY: Well, it's a business relationship. I mean the vendors get their money from their customers who are usually corporates, and the corporates get their protection from the vendors—that's why it's a market. It's a mutually beneficial relationship.

Corporates get protection from vendors, and through this business relationship, corporates are seen to exercise the consequential power of choice over vendors. It is suggested that this type of market relationship equalizes the corporate customers' technological dependency—it is 'mutually beneficial'. Corporate customers can choose which vendor they want protection from, which vendor meets their needs. The vendors see themselves as correspondingly dependent on corporate customers for monetary support. Vendors suggest they seek out 'corporate' opinions and needs in order to more effectively produce a responsive product. In this way, vendors suggest the needs of the corporate end users are strategically integrated with the vendors' goals. They describe the relationship as 'mutual' and 'both ways', seemingly delegating aspects of product development initiatives to their corporate customers. It is a mutually beneficial business relationship conducted on a neutral level playing field within a market economy.

Critique of Consumer Choice

It is too simplistic, however, to celebrate consumerist choice, the mutually beneficial relationship, or 'the compromise', without a concomitant analysis of the socially constrained nature of that choice. One vendor, who left the antivirus industry soon after the interview, comments about the power relations inherent in technological innovations within the industry:

> VENDOR TIMOTHY: It seems to me that there's a disconnect between the companies and their customers. In general, customers buy the products that are available. You can't buy anything else. The companies get to decide what products are available. If they make the wrong thing, the customers won't buy it anyway because it's rubbish. So there's a feedback thing going on here. And where we've ended up in antivirus anyway is . . . we've all settled on scanners. That's all anyone knows of basically. We don't know anything other than scanners. Now that could be because of several reasons. It could be because that's what the customers want. Or, it could be because what the customers want is all that there is. Or, it could be because it's the best answer.

The 'disconnect' this vendor articulates challenges the concept of integrated, mutually beneficial relationships and equitable compromises between vendors and their customers. Reflective of most industries within a capitalist economy, antivirus vendors' conceptualizations of the need of their corporate customers is based on what they have gathered from 'feedback'. Within the antivirus industry, vendors continually say their corporate customers tell them what they want, through their sales personnel or customer forums devised for that purpose. This feedback generates a pattern, a synthesis of their specific customer's wants and needs. This synthesized information is then given back to the corporate customer in the form of viable product options. Yet this synthesized information was set by the original production values. Customers have the ability to give feedback on a limited set of options. Those options then reinforce the feedback about the original technological selections available. The conceptualization generated through this limited feedback normalizes the requests of the corporate customer. Scanners remain the only option because 'that's all anyone knows'. Other options are not available for consideration within the feedback loop. The system is open to the extent that it can absorb what fits into the already established pattern. The options available reinforce that pattern and the cycle begins again.

In essence, the vendors define and construct antivirus technology within their own parameters using cost effective strategies and plans. Corporate end users utilize the antivirus products that are available to protect their corporate sites, actively implementing and adapting them into their sites, creatively developing their strategies and own workarounds on the products provided.

The nature of commerce is stacked against the isolated and individualized corporate end user. He must work within the already established structures, where he is always power poor, seen as technically deficient, as inconsistently requesting the impossible, his contributions to the process seemingly invisible. This framework generates corporate customers only requesting innovations that make sense to the vendors, that are 'common sense'.

CORPORATE END USER EARL: I think that we are reasonably sensible in what we ask for. And if they can see the sense in it, and then they can see other customers also asking for the same thing, then it makes sense. It's common sense. They will then do it.

This corporate end user projects his vendor's perception of 'common sense', and requests only that. The customer requests that will be addressed are only those that are seen by the vendors as 'reasonable' and 'sensible'. But who determines these qualities? If vendors hear and see other corporate customers making similar requests, then vendors might also consider their combined requirements. But how many 'others' does it take to reach that magic threshold? I asked a researcher:

RESEARCHER MICHAEL: Sometimes when the suggestions are made by corporates, we even give them that particular solution to try out as well. But until the magic threshold is reached on a type-particular suggestion, we really can't incorporate one person's suggestion into ours, because the person that makes the suggestion, even if it is a good suggestion, he is only one customer. We have to balance it out.

I: Right. How do you know when that magic threshold has been reached?

RESEARCHER MICHAEL: You know, sometimes it's because that one customer is big enough to have gotten to one of our upper levels who thinks, you know, shit rolls downhill [laughs]. If they can catch the right person up top, we're forced to do something based on one customer. Sometimes it's because we've heard the same suggestion from a number of people. And, you know, one way of measuring it is, should you just do it? Or should you keep on answering the same question? For instance, the movement toward addressing Trojans in our antivirus products was partly manifested because it's a lot easier to do it than it is to tell them, "Actually that's not a virus, and dadadadada. . . ." They say, "But I want it." And you say, "Okay, I guess I'll just do it" and not have to waste five minutes for every single person who's going to come up to me and you know.

'Corporates' are isolated individuals, continually asking, one by one, for what vendors consider inappropriate and misinformed product 'improvements'. By approaching a researcher 'every five minutes' and asking for erroneous types of malware protections, each corporate is seen as wasting this researcher's time. But if they are big enough and powerful enough, they might be able to have an effect. The 'magic threshold' is amorphous, and as such is swayed by negotiated relationships within a capitalist economy.

Accepted technological innovation is reified and naturalized through this type of consumer market orientation. Power is wielded, masked as 'common sense'. Obscured through this process are the power relations between vendors and corporate end users, as the technological hierarchies are reinforced and reproduced. Within the antivirus industry, the creation of common sense and accepted knowledge is focused through both this technological hierarchy and a consumer market. Together, both of these standpoints authoritatively define the industry's power relationships. While both the vendors' and their corporate customers' perspectives reveal their diverse social locations, from the corporate end users' viewpoint, the vendors' position is endowed with common sense and 'reality'. Conversely, corporates' needs, unless seen as shared by other customers, are (re)presented as outside the acceptable bounds of rational sense, and are thus irritating and thought by some within the industry to be 'idiotic'.

Corporate end users are isolated as individual consumers. They remain polite and silenced. They have difficulty addressing technological issues unless a consensus is recognized. The corporate end users' input is identified, by both vendors and the corporate end users, simultaneously as an established practice and a contested terrain. Yet the corporate end users' issues remain nonissues, and do not become a part of the vendors' agendas unless they can all speak with one voice.

Corporate End Users as Consumer Group

Realizing both their dependency and the combined power of that one voice, corporate end users began to overtly seek other corporate IT administrators in similar situations, and together define their claims. Grouping together allowed them to actively resist their market-induced passivity and vulnerability, defined as 'non-technical' users. As corporate end users of isolated businesses, many felt dependent and powerless. However, as a networked body of large and small businesses with similar needs and perspectives, they realized a voice that acknowledged the driving forces behind the vendors' market imperatives. By speaking with one voice they transformed their needs into their vendors' economically 'rational' or commonsense innovations. In creating a power base of numerical significance, a power base that could no longer be ignored or invalidated, they negotiated with the vendors' market-based imperatives. By grouping together they could counter the perceived neglect of the industry.

> CORPORATE END USER EARL: I go to a 'council meeting', as they are called with the vendors. They have them, you know, on a regular basis and I talk to them about my own requirements. But then I work with other corporations and we all then bend the ear of the vendor, and so we have a greater voice. And the individual organization, even with the large licensing that we have, we can only influence them a certain degree. But when you have everybody else involved and you are then talking in hundreds, well not hundreds of millions, but certainly, probably fifty million-plus licenses sort of thing, then you start sort of having quite a lot of sway with them.

These vendor-sponsored 'council meetings' allow the individualized corporate end user the ability to talk with the vendor. Vendors suggest that users participate in design meetings and decision platforms, arguing that the resulting technologies are a successful iterative process. Vendors and their researchers positioned their customers in this easy, open, mutually reciprocal business relationship, assuming the consumer role gives power to the corporate end users. But as suggested in the quote above, this supposed influential role and communication forum is problematic. Divisions and their inherent power relationships still remain. Individually 'chatting' with the vendors does not guarantee that any of the technological innovations are integrated into the antivirus product. Corporate end users as individual customers cannot 'bend the ear' of the vendor. It is only when the corporate end users work together with their fifty million-plus licenses that they have an effect. As a block of consumers, they ask questions of how different 'needs' and 'services' are defined, and how, and by whom, organizational objectives are set and pursued. The conflicting images of corporate end users inherent in their technological and consumer roles, being technologically dependent yet acknowledging their combined power within a consumer economy, allows these corporate users, as a consumer block, greater voice and influence within the industry.

The fact that the antivirus industry is composed of multiple-situated and conflicting knowledges, and that these worlds are represented and experienced in different, and often competing, ways has significant implications for antivirus technology (Klein and Kleinman 2002). The three segments within the antivirus industry—researchers, vendors, and the 'corporate people'—inevitably struggle over definitions and classifications about what the software should be and should do. Contestations over recognizing 'Bob's and Jane's' technological capabilities, the amount and type of communication between vendors and corporate end users, and the role of corporate end users as customers compel the 'corporate people' to share and collaborate on their collective confusion. Indeed, corporate end users are placed within multiple double-binds. As customers, they are expected to politely ask for what they need, to contribute to the iterative process, but are negated for not respecting or appreciating vendors' innovative insights and expertise. Corporate end users can 'choose' technology and antivirus vendors through their purchases, however, they cannot dictate the technology. The communication between vendor and the corporate customer is supposedly a compromise between equals and a mutually beneficial market relationship. Interpreted in this way, their collaboration is a form of democratic design that supposedly allows everyone to have a voice in the development of the technology. But not everyone is heard. Many corporate end users remain invisible and silenced, mere irritants without respect. The technology is both established and altered by these double-binds and their inherent conflicts and silences.

AVIEN—'The Corporates' Network

The corporate end users' awareness of their combined economic power in the struggle over antivirus software developed into an official organization. AVIEN, the Anti-Virus Information Exchange Network, is another exclusive organization dedicated to electronic exchange of information, but this one is a group of corporate end users. In 2000, a group of corporate end users at a computer virus conference began a conversation about forming a networked discussion list of their own. They wanted to share information among themselves that was applicable to their corporate sites. Provoked by their exclusion from other malware discussion e-lists, they formed their own online forum. The AVIEN Web site states:

> For many years, security specialists around the world working to defend their organizations against attacks from viruses, worms, and other forms of malware had essentially two choices if they wanted to learn more about this topic: work in relative isolation or be invited to join a vendor-oriented group. The vendor-oriented groups (CARO, REVS, VForum, AVPD,[3] etc.) were designed from the beginning to respond to the need to share information, but membership was usually restricted to those who worked for a software vendor or occasional corporate employees and university researchers who were invited to join to share their insights. For the vast majority of specialists working in large organizations on malware defense, there was little hope of entering that circle.
>
> (AVIEN—Anti-Virus Information Exchange Network)

AVIEN originated to counter the corporate end users' isolation and exclusion from the global information and communication structures of the antivirus researchers and vendors. While being somewhat 'inside' the industry—they are the corporate customers and hands-on organizational specialists using the antivirus products—they were still excluded from antivirus discussion lists as merely the ignorant 'Bob and Jane' end users of the antivirus products.

As members of AVIEN, however, these corporate end users came to see themselves as a unique community and use AVIEN as an information network to provide alternatives and solutions to their technological dependency. Celebrating their outsider status, they confronted the symbolic authority and the information monopoly of the other antivirus groups' inner circles. A corporate end user from a large transnational corporation states:

---

[3] VForum originally was a 'feeder' for potential CARO members. It has been transformed into more of an industry-wide discussion list, though joining the list is still 'by invitation only'. AVPD is an antivirus vendor consortium, run by the International Computer Security Association (ICSA), which focuses on antivirus product certification (http://www.icsalabs.com/).

CORPORATE END USER CHRIS: I feel like it's—from my standpoint as a customer in the industry, I think AVIEN is the best thing that's ever happened to the communication from my level. Because there is definitely a lack of getting information to those of us in the field, those of us you know, trying to protect our company. We weren't given information in a timely manner at all, even if it was from our own vendors.

AVIEN members, as the corporate customers in the antivirus industry, supply a seemingly necessary network for communication, specifically relevant to corporate end users' needs and goals. They see vendors, even their 'own vendors', as not responding appropriately or in a suitable time frame, leaving these managers who are responsible for their corporate systems, both dependent upon and vulnerable to their vendors' information disclosures. Instead, AVIEN gathers together all those 'in the field', all those dealing with the actual threats to their daily networked flow of information. Through discussion based on their social location 'in the field', AVIEN allows corporate end users to more effectively exchange information and gauge current and evolving threats to their corporation's security.

As we have seen with both CARO and REVS in the preceding chapter, networks of information reflect and influence social boundaries. Exclusive networks have the ability, through inclusion and exclusion, to clearly define and reproduce seemingly distinct perceptions and social realities. AVIEN members construct their struggle as one of hierarchical control—a type of class struggle. They are the alternative, democratic grassroots community, an organization of like-minded, vulnerable yet informed and committed corporate end users. They challenge the rationality of CARO's position and exclusive influence over the industry. Indeed, AVIEN constructs itself within this hierarchy as 'on the front line', highlighting the contrast between those who deal with the real-world consequences to the threats on a daily, even hourly, basis, and the 'experts' who are attempting to maintain the hierarchy yet are removed from those real-world consequences. A corporate end user articulates this gap as he describes his job:

CORPORATE END USER CHRIS: And now, and more often than not, we're the ones that are seeing things first and so it's—

bottom line, my job is to protect my company and that's my priority. I need to know what I can do, whether it's something proactive or just mitigate something until there's protection in place. I need to know that. AVIEN gives me that option now, because—and it's given me a communication tool that did not exist. It's just opened up I think a lot of exchange that needed to be done. Now there's obviously two sides to AVIEN, there's the side that the vendors aren't allowed in where we just, we don't trash vendors obviously, but we do a lot of talking and there's a lot of e-mail. Believe me, I can't always get to it all.

AVIEN maximizes the responsiveness for this corporate end user. His bottom line is to protect his company's IT infrastructure. From his perspective, if his company's technological infrastructure is attacked, he is the one 'seeing things first' in the fast-changing environment. Being 'first' in this sense is transformed for the AVIEN member. Being 'first' in an attack becomes a point of information, not a position of vulnerability and dependency. 'Seeing things first' is transformed into a position of power and knowledge, and is contextualized as preceding all others in the exchange of information. 'Seeing things first' means first *before his vendor*. With this empowered position, all corporate sites in AVIEN become potential global network sensors, feeding their current status alerts into AVIEN as the hub. They no longer merely wait for their vendors to tell them what to do, what actions they should take. Reacting to 'seeing things first' and being 'in the field' are highlighted over waiting for the top-down approach from CARO researchers and their vendors.

Because of the exchange of information within their integrated network, AVIEN thus allows all participating corporate end users to act and respond. They can open or close sections of their corporate networks and adapt in accordance with the relevant and current information being circulated. AVIEN permits the reintegration of these information sites into an informed decision-making process of all, and *for* all, participating corporate end users. This exchanged information permits flexibility and coordination, ensuring innovative strategies in an evolving threatening environment. AVIEN members see themselves as a real-time, dynamic, strategic network of self-programmed, self-directed units based on information, participation, and communication.

Significantly, AVIEN excludes vendors and researchers from its discussion group. AVIEN developed its own communication channel to collaboratively and proactively respond to immediate threats, and as a counterpoint to the lack of communication from vendors and vendors' product solutions. While 'corporates' are still dependent on vendors for protection software, in a sense, AVIEN reorders the flow of information about an outbreak. Techniques of domination exercised by the vendors are subverted and utilized by AVIEN as practices of resistance. By developing its own exclusive information exchange, by projecting it into the official dialogue as a collaborative voice, there is a kind of strategic reversibility of the power relationships. AVIEN transforms the corporates' sense of dependency and exclusion into a united, collaborative, and legitimate position for negotiations. As such, AVIEN became a recognized player in the dynamic interaction between the various antivirus networks as well as a factor in the shape of technological innovations.

Within AVIEN, a sense of community is achieved across its divergent global corporate members with varied if not antithetical business orientations. The uncertainties in the goals to protect both the network and their corporate sites combine to articulate a common direction of struggle. In any decision of importance, they seek out each other's opinions and current and past experiences, deconstructing vendors' messages, exploring other end users' views, looking out for fellow end users. They use their information exchange to obtain the views of many as global sensors, as a social network, and as a guide to decision making. Their networked communication becomes their trusted authority. Through their participation and through discussion of various options with their peers they become more informed antivirus specialists, more aware corporate customers, more able to prevent infections within their own corporate IT infrastructure, and thus more able to prevent the global spread of contagion to other corporations on the network. They are no longer merely reacting, but are now active players within the antivirus industry.

While in some ways upturning the technological hierarchy, AVIEN also underscores the real-world significance of this membership group as a power block of informed corporate customers. AVIEN as a virtual networked group of mutually informed consumers yields a new entity that is more powerful than is possible for any of the participants acting alone. Their strength is linked to their networked ability to exclusively exchange their secret and private information and to distill their demands and expectations into institutional provisions. Networking together allows these corporate end users to move from feeling dependent and technologically disadvantaged toward the reality of sovereign customers impacting the direction of the industry. This corporate end user discusses AVIEN's power base:

> CORPORATE END USER STEVEN: I don't see a problem with it. I mean I can see why the antivirus industry may not like it because it, ah, gets a bunch of people together and gives them power. What does AVIEN say? It has, you know, five million PCs. That is support folks! It is five million PCs! Maybe it's more than that now, you know! You say, look, you know, we actually have some buying power here, leverage. We can say we are not going to buy your product unless you do this. And as far as I know they haven't actually done that. But having that as a threat over the industry, I'm sure doesn't make them happy, especially the vendors.

The 'leverage' of five million PCs is seen by those both inside and outside AVIEN as giving weight and strength to the corporate end users' position within the industry. Instead of being invisible as individualized end users, they have the power inherent within a market economy. They can act as a block of informed and collaborative corporate consumers.

AVIEN members continually contrast their inclusive grassroots appeal and their organization's communal and supportive structure against CARO's hierarchical, exclusive, technical expertise. While AVIEN identifies itself as oppositional to CARO, however, it also shares three important structural qualities. First, similar to CARO, AVIEN draws members from across conventional competitors. AVIEN is a worldwide information exchange network that intersects the seeming boundaries between businesses of various types and sizes with vastly different products and business strategies. In AVIEN's case, this cross-border structure allows corporate end users from local businesses to link up with major global corporations, forming networks that are able to innovate and progressively adapt to the evolving and fast-paced development of outbreaks. AVIEN's structure permits the simultaneously decentralized gathering and retrieval of information and its integration into a flexible 'early warning system' for all AVIEN members. This highly diverse set of corporate end users communicates across time, space, and corporate sites, consolidating all their information for retrieval by everyone. Like CARO, AVIEN's use of internet communication structures helps them transgress traditional boundaries in order to form strategies to deal with both virus threats and computer security vendors.

A second similarity between AVIEN and CARO is that AVIEN members attribute the success of AVIEN to its development of 'community'. Like CARO's 'band of brothers' and beer-drinking techie friends, AVIEN has developed a connectedness that is consistently identified by its members as integral to its success.

> CORPORATE END USER KEVIN: It's a community. AVIEN is now an online community. It went from being just a group of people talking to each other occasionally to being an actual online community. You know, people get very emotional about what we are doing, and what we are saying, and how people are responding and that sort of thing.

AVIEN developed a close network of people who share technical information, industry perspectives, and friendships across the barriers of competitive corporate entities. AVIEN transgresses the boundaries of corporate identities with participants understanding how their companies' assets are directly linked with others in the flow of networked information. The link between their own company's connectivity and their competitors' connectivity is recognized as entwined. AVIEN developed from merely warning others about spikes and networked attacks into a shared community of like-minded people. The online 'community' is central to the corporate end users' perspective of their AVIEN identity.

Third, similar to CARO, AVIEN's networks of information exchange also act as a gatekeeper. The three-tiered social separation within the industry between researchers, vendors, and corporate end users is technically reproduced and maintained in the official exclusion of non-AVIEN members. In AVIEN's case, even though it is a grass-roots organization and rejects the CARO hierarchy, it too limits its membership. No vendors or antivirus researchers are allowed on the list. And only businesses that have over 1,500 personal computers (PCs) on site are allowed to join. AVIEN reproduces an exclusive virtual space where only large corporate users can discuss malware issues applicable to their corporate needs. An AVIEN member comments about the vendors' attitude toward the origins of AVIEN:

> CORPORATE END USER KEVIN: The vendors were very worried at the beginning. They thought that we were out to bash them, or to cause problems for them, or you know, just to complain about them, just kind of like bitching, whatever. The reality is that occasionally people would put a push in and say oh, you know, "This product is causing me so much grief." Usually the response you get from someone else will be, "Well, have you tried this?" "Oh you mean I can fix this? Well why didn't the vendor tell me that?" "Well, who knows, you know, this is how I figured it out," or, "I got this information but it's not generally available yet." Or, whatever.

Within AVIEN's network, not only do they act as frontline network sensors, they also share information about both their own corporations and the antivirus products at their corporate sites. They too have secret information that they want to exclude from nonmembers. In the desire to share only with and learn from other corporate end users, AVIEN members feel the need to protect secret information gathered through their communications about their various corporate structures. AVIEN then is structurally similar to CARO in many of its organizational foundations. AVIEN's community crosses traditional corporate borders and desires to protect information by excluding other segments of the industry.

AVIEN's desire to exclude and segregate itself from others within the antivirus industry generated animosity from vendors. AVIEN members responded with the creation of another virtual discussion group, AVIEWS, or the Anti-Virus Information Early Warning System.

CORPORATE END USER CHRIS: There was a lot of animosity from the vendors' side. So we created a site for the vendors to join in, the Anti-Virus Information Early Warning System. I don't know why do they join—I don't know if they saw how useful a tool it is. The thing is, all the vendors have their little information-sharing forums, be it CARO or what-have-you, and it's so exclusive. But it doesn't help me to protect my company. It doesn't help me with any kind of communication, whereas AVIEN does. AVIEN met a huge need for us.

Vendors and researchers are seen to have their own 'little information-sharing forums' like CARO that exclude the 'corporate people'. In 2002, AVIEN began another related online discussion community that allows vendors, researchers, small business and corporate end users, journalists, product testers, and so on to join. For a cost of a year's subscription, any antivirus industry professional is allowed to participate. Based on AVIEN's ability to be a virtual communication network for large corporate users, AVIEWS is established.

CORPORATE END USER KEVIN: AVIEN is all the users got together to talk. AVIEWS is when we open the door and said that the vendors can join us. The vendors kept coming and saying, "We want to be part of this," and we would have to say, "Well, you can't. You know you've got CARO, we've got AVIEN." Basically I would see things and I would then go back to the list and say, "Look, the vendors want in." "We don't want them in." So with AVIEWS, for the first time, the vendors, and most of the major vendors are in there, although some participate more than others—and I don't know what the rationale is at that level, but anyway— is that you have got customers and you have got vendors talking in an open forum. Until that happened, what you had was the vendors talking one-on-one with the customers. They'd have their 'user forums', right, where they would get their customers together and talk with them and, you know, wine and dine them and basically hope that

they didn't get too out of line and ask for too many things.
In this case, it's people talking openly. Now they talk mainly
about threats and how to deal with them and viruses and
that sort of thing. They don't talk a lot about products and
stuff, but they do, you know, do a bit of product stuff.

AVIEWS was created by AVIEN members to allow vendors and
other antivirus industry professionals a forum for open discussion.
Previously, vendors had 'user forums' where vendors would talk directly with just their corporate end users. These corporate end users,
however, rarely talked with each other, and would be managed so they
would not 'get too out of line' and 'ask for too many things'. Corporate
end users, denigrated as 'Bob and Jane from accounts', were treated as
novices and non-experts. With the growth of AVIEN and its expansion
into AVIEWS, the relations between the users and producers of
antivirus technologies were renegotiated. Through AVIEN and
AVIEWS, corporate users have more direct engagement in the construction of the industry's technologies. Instead of a one-way flow of
information, where the user is told not to ask for 'too much', vendors
and the 'corporate people' have the potential to discuss problems and
solutions in real time.

AVIEWS is a good example, however, of how individuals can be
components of multiple and sometimes competing or antithetical networks that are aimed at divergent goals and priorities. Based on their
social location within the industry, researchers and vendors bring to
AVIEWS their own specific goals that appropriate this 'open forum'
into another marketing opportunity.

RESEARCHER MICHAEL: We have people who are involved in
the other groups that are also associated with AVIEN-
AVIEWS—where they allow contributors from AV companies. I think that any direct connection from those admins
as a group to AV researchers is a good thing. It allows us to
broadcast on a lot more personal level and be able to respond to questions. It is something where the researchers
can get input from the users a lot quicker, and also be
involved in a sort of technological race between the researchers when they recognize from the users, "Well, this

is what they really want, let's see what we can do." And do that, rather than forcing the customers to go through the salespeople who may lose some sort of interaction or some sort of interpretation.

Researchers as vendors' employees use AVIEWS to softly market their antivirus products. It allows researchers and vendors to 'broadcast' on a 'more personal level', putting them more directly in touch with their corporate customers. AVIEWS provides researchers and vendors with the opportunity for a many-to-many dialogue, with input from the corporate users generating technical 'races' between researchers. By demonstrating concern for users, this researcher suggests they also do impression management, generating a more customer and end user focus. By participating, they also can decipher more directly what customers want. For vendors then, the information exchanged in AVIEWS allows the straightforward communication between the corporate end users' perspective and experiences in order that the vendors and researchers can learn, adapt, and respond more quickly. AVIEWS helps them adapt in the competitive marketplace.

For vendors, AVIEWS is another channel in the relentless production and marketing of antivirus software. The information gathered there is transformed into market advantages, allowing vendors an 'inside track' to the corporate end users' combined perspectives and needs. Instead of AVIEWS being a 'community' of antivirus professionals, vendors incorporate the discussion into consumer capitalism. It provides information for a technical race between researchers rather than an open examination of the inequalities of industry power. The dissatisfaction and rebellion that propelled the growth of AVIEN is redefined for venders in AVIEWS as a new avenue of commodity production. AVIEWS becomes the vendors' lucrative resource and a tool in the commodification of information.

How these different socially-situated professionals deal with the threats to the internet reveal their various professional alliances within the industry. The fragmentation into their various information exchange networks reproduces their institutional boundaries. CARO began in order to share dangerous knowledge exclusively among antivirus research specialists regardless of their employers. REVS began in order to allow vendors to share knowledge without dependencies on

CARO researchers. AVIEN began as a grassroots effort to share knowledge exclusively among corporate end users barred from REVS and CARO. AVIEWS began so as to reverse the lack of communication established between these privatized information networks.

While their various information exchange networks compete and generate distance by flexing and pulling these professionals in seemingly opposing directions, they also generate new alliances between them. While AVIEWS celebrates its inclusiveness, it is still used by vendors, researchers, and corporate end users to push their own agendas. CARO, REVS, AVIEN, and AVIEWS are the consequences generated by the fast-paced spread of global communication, and the historical and seemingly rational decisions inherent in the development of the antivirus industry that supports that communication. All these discussion lists create a hierarchy of various knowledge systems that excludes others because of their social location and their corresponding knowledges and priorities within the antivirus industry. The flexibly networked work associations, however, also generate new networks, new knowledges, and new technological innovations.

As technology changes, so too do the threats and types of protection for digital networks. AVIEN and AVIEWS promoted themselves as early warning systems, as the 'front line' of attacks to the internet. However, this primary function for the industry is challenged. Vendors align with 'service providers', such as MessageLabs, as 'the' original frontline thoroughfare of most globally networked communication. AVIEN's and AVIEWS's relevance is questioned by a researcher:

> RESEARCHER WILLIAM: As an early warning system, I don't see any value because usually the people who are sending out the warnings are the vendors and we already get them. So, for instance, you have MessageLabs alerting on something they spot more often and they have stopped so many copies in the last hour. By that time they already have sent all the AV vendors samples of those copies before that. So we already are working on it.

Vendors adapted their strategies of information gathering by working through service providers like MessageLabs, a company that developed specifically to filter networked viruses and spam. The frontline authority inherent in the 'sensors' of service providers relaying information to vendors in real time cannot be matched by AVIEN. AVIEN's importance remains located within the corporate end users' shared communications systems. While they are still an early warning system to other corporate end users, they are not vendors' or researchers' global sensors.

Power and knowledge are always contested and dynamic, in this case they are dependent on the evolution of network flows and activities processed through the network. The constantly changing environment of high technology combined with consolidation of service providers prevents one of AVIEN's central claims to industry legitimacy from becoming a more influential communication function. Technological changes correspond with the amalgamation of internet traffic into mammoth ISPs as power blocks. Vendors adjust to these transformations, protecting both the internet and their social authority in a market economy. Information coming from a specific time and space continues to be the crucial factor. However, the large service providers are the ultimate sensors critical to vendors' measurement of internet traffic and spikes in the information flow. ISPs are specifically constructed to process and move internet traffic, unencumbered by extraneous corporate missions. ISPs are the current circulators of information.

In this sense, antivirus software is never closed or stabilized (Klein and Kleinman 2002; Orlikowski and Barley 2001). ISPs currently monitor spam, denial of service, and other related malware attacks. Antivirus software is continually assessed, critiqued, explained, worked-around, and redesigned in response to inputs from antivirus industry professionals, new technological innovations, and new threats from spam, spim,[4] and vulnerabilities on cell phones. Changes in technology have ripple effects, transforming relations and positions within the antivirus industry. These transformations in technology result in shifts in information flow that then affect existing competencies and knowledge structures. The transformation in the hierarchical ordering of positions within the industry has flow-on effects and results in new technological innovations, which then affect these social alliances in a never-ending cycle.

---

[4] 'Spim' is a recently coined term for 'spam sent via instant messenger (IM) services'.

Evolving Power Relationships, Situated Ethics, and Secrecy

Historical evolution of the antivirus industry is an open-ended, conflictive process, enacted by various socially-situated professionals.
Compared to the computer viruses encountered by 'first generation'
antivirus specialists and the original milieu of academic experiments
or games in the computer labs, the technical evolution and dynamic
expansion of antivirus software has created a qualitatively new context
of threats in its implementation of 'security'. Over the six years of the
interviews, there were corresponding challenges to the definition of
what is a threat and who or what is a security risk within the antivirus
industry. The historical and cultural making and unmaking of CARO,
REVS, and AVIEN affected understandings of what internet security
is, both as a technology and a social practice.

Within this social and technological context of evolving threats,
fiercely contested ethical and technological judgments were made between CARO, REVS, and AVIEN as to what constitutes the appropriate use of computer resources. The purported basis and subsequent
maintenance of this hostility is part of a boundary-forming process
whereby each group reaffirms their own identity and legitimacy by
marginalizing others. The rationale for their various privatized information exchanges was to protect information from malicious code
writers. The stated purpose of their exclusive boundary formation processes was grounded in preventing the malicious code writer from
gaining access to industry secrets. However, the purpose expands out
to generalized industry 'others' attempting to discipline and contain
them, while simultaneously developing a consistent ethical value system for 'legitimate' antivirus professionals. Focus on the malicious
code writer or his technological misdeeds is sidelined. The 'white hat'
versus 'black hat' battle becomes somewhat secondary, as the antivirus
industry labors simultaneously to develop and enforce internal industry standards and objectives.

The antivirus industry is then an interlocking system of competing knowledges, representations, practices, institutions, and technical
forms. An amalgamation of the continual contestations between these
knowledges, the industry imagines, directs, and acts upon the information and the technological products that protect information. As a way

of building strategic alliances, their forums transform the industry as people respond to both the information generated and the inclusiveness and exclusiveness of the processes. Inherent in the process of exchanging information is the repercussion of what is kept from others. This paradox of 'keeping while giving' determines insider and outsider status, affecting the corresponding social, cultural, and economic capitals of each forum. Exchanged information then becomes a scarce resource as it excludes and privatizes its processes and results. Exclusion from any of these insider networks curtails effectiveness and makes survival within the industry difficult. Conflict over these scarce resources must be continually renegotiated as technological transformations affect the industry, the threats, and the technology itself.

The contrast between CARO's, REVS's, and AVIEN's interpretation of their positions within the antivirus industry demonstrates that technological security is never neutral or individualistic. It is always shaped through anxieties and the resultant contestations that extend beyond 'technology' and the rubric of 'threat', and is about controlling and containing the 'other' whether it is the virus writer or other industry groups. Within the antivirus industry, each membership group develops in response to and against previous exclusive exchanges. Each membership group is an attempt to compensate for another's contradictory rhetorical and material practices. The question of who can determine who is legitimate and trustworthy, or who is a security risk is answered differently by each and changes over time, highlighting the changing power relations in the industry. Over time, some institutional structures and networks of power are reified, their security enunciations empowering their members to speak about security in a specific way. Their exchange networks are thus entrenched in institutionalized patterns of technological practices, simultaneously empowering and constraining these industry professionals in terms of how, and how powerfully, they can affect the technology involved in internet security.

Secrecy plays a crucial role in the antivirus industry's knowledge production. Secrecy shrouds all their privatized information exchanges, ultimately veiling information from the malicious code writers, but also from unworthy others within the industry. Each membership group cultivates a sort of competence in their perspective and use of antivirus technology, becoming an elite group with their own special authority, knowledge, and experience. Each group believes it should be granted authority and recognition by those who have no such competence, creating competing knowledge monopolies. Having control over the workings of a particular socially-situated perspective of antivirus technology, they accumulate power and inevitably form a knowledge monopoly against those who have no access to their specialized knowledge. Through their various communication networks, information exchange for each appears to their members to be unique and superior, while simultaneously negating the others. Their use of secrecy reproduces their different social locations within the industry, while simultaneously reinforcing their need to deliberately withhold their exclusive knowledge and information from others. All articulate their access to the secret information through discourses of morality and elitism. Secret information then both reproduces and challenges the inherent structural inequalities and separations that circulate around the power/knowledge nexus.

Power is messy. It is nebulous, needs continual protection, renegotiation, and alliances. Sources of job security and status hierarchies, whether an IT corporate administrator or a top-level elite antivirus researcher, are based on the manipulation of information. That information fuses capitalism with science and technology, merges ethics with issues of financial security, and shrouds the communication of knowledge with secrecy and apprehension, all combine to effect the definitions of threat and technological security within the antivirus industry.

5 Marketing Service

Service Metaphors

Antivirus (AV) industry professionals, whether researcher, vendor, or corporate end user, see themselves as both protecting technology and providing for the common good of the global networked community. They situate themselves in the 'white hat–black hat' contestation against virus writers, with their roles as benevolent experts and protectors opposing the cyber thieves and malicious code writers. They construct themselves as having a service relationship to the world, with a duty and an ethical responsibility to work against the virus writer to create a secure environment for electronic communications. They continually articulate their duty to safeguard technological infrastructures, and express altruistic and supportive attitudes as integral to the service orientation of the industry.

> RESEARCHER KEITH: Our objective is to prevent things from breaking as much as possible, to get detection as early as possible, to get it out there before whatever the latest threat is, gets to someone's machine so it can be detected and blocked on the way in, rather than getting in and causing the problem that then has to be cleaned up. But, you

know, the fact that we are trying to do that preemptively, it is still a service. It is very much a service industry now. Very, very strongly for a very, very long time I have said that.

These antivirus professionals take pride in the service they provide. Antivirus is as much about the actual technology as it is about the social relations of providing support to others. Many identified the appeal of their work as revolving around helping people protect themselves, their homes, businesses, and communities, thus placing a barrier in the path of the criminal other. Antivirus products are seen to make a real-world contribution toward living and working in a safer, more secure technological environment.

Several recurring service metaphors were used to directly compare the industry with other caregiving professions. Antivirus professionals continually cited the same service professions as descriptive analogies of their work:

RESEARCHER CHARLES: I think firefighting is the most useful analogy because you have to solve a problem quickly or it will spread. In AV, and to some extent in malware, the only problem is that the firefighting industry has a very good backup in terms of fire prevention. Fire prevention is something that is not done by AV people. It is done by ordinary administrators who certainly won't have a feel for the next virus coming along.

VENDOR RONALD: I think we are actually pretty much fulfilling the role of a cyber police officer, as much as that can be fulfilled. It's not like we work for cigarette companies or even like, you know, alcohol companies, or something like that, where. . . . And I think in this, at least the intent of the industry, although you know sometimes the execution can be sort of somewhat skewed, but the intent of the industry is certainly very honorable. And I think that's why a lot of people tend to stay in it for a while.

Besides firefighters and police, other metaphorical service occupations repeatedly mentioned were doctors, biologists, pharmacists, and lifeguards. The basic intention espoused by most industry professionals did not involve money or developing the biggest antivirus company. Instead, the driving force behind the industry was the passion and the desire to create something socially valuable. Their dedication to their end users is seen to emerge out of a responsive humanitarian and philanthropic orientation. The antivirus industry is there to protect and serve.

Similar to firefighters, pharmacists, lifeguards, police, and doctors, they are experts in their field with specialist knowledge that is used for the betterment of others. And while they are concerned with the technical aspects of antivirus, they also see themselves as responsive to the needs of the computer user. Fusing the social and the technological, their knowledge is not directed toward exploitive or merely commercial 'mindless' products, but is used to serve the networked community. Recognizing the importance of computers as repositories of negotiable assets and computer networks as a vital conduit for transmitting information, they protect the confidentiality, availability, and integrity of data. They take pride in their 'honorable' profession.

The Profit Motive of the Antivirus Industry

There is, however, conflict. This service ethos, with its corresponding priorities and activities, conflicts with many of the financial and administrative strategies that are needed to support it. Ultimately, the vocabulary and objectives of a consumption economy dominate much of the antivirus industry's service discourse.

I: Is there a conflict between saving the world from malicious code and making a profit?

RESEARCHER MICHAEL: Conflict? There is short-term conflict. In the long run you, you're building a trust empire and if you . . . people will recognize in the long run that you've been, you've had their best interests at heart, and so forth. So, um, in the long run there's no conflict. But sometimes it's hard to get that far with all the quarterly requirements.

I: So, is it a balance? Or do you see the industry being controlled by one more than the other?

RESEARCHER MICHAEL: Um [long pause] I think money always has control.

There is a fundamental and deep-seated contradiction over service and profit. Antivirus is a profit industry. Having clients' 'best interests at heart' may be the long term objective, but the commercial imperative reigns supreme. Selling software, maximizing profits, and providing a return for investors is recognized by most as ultimately having more influence on the direction of the industry than service and protection. The antivirus industry's service values, unbiased scientific roots, and technological ingenuity are coopted by corporate concerns and 'all those quarterly requirements'. The balance between stimulating production, and servicing and protecting the public must be continually negotiated and renegotiated as information is commodified and increasingly geared toward high-paying markets. Cost-effectiveness is seen as ultimately determining technological development, not the need to provide protection and security. According to this researcher, "money always has control."

The effect of the service–profit conflict creates radical doubts about the antivirus industry's service discourse. The contradiction undercuts the belief that the industry offers technical knowledge that is 'innocent' or neutral, unconnected to a profit margin. The calculation of supply and demand is usually formed as a question about the industry's ability to survive without artificially supplementing or actually supplying computer viruses in order to make a profit:

> RESEARCHER DANIEL: If you ask the 'man in the street', he will always think that we are making viruses in order to create demand for our products. Goodness knows that we are overloaded with viruses made by virus writers and we don't need any more work! But this is what people think, that it would really be in our interest to create viruses. This is going to horribly damage our reputation. People will stop trusting us, and stop trusting our products. And in the end it will hurt the users too because if they are not going to use our products, they are not going to be protected. Why don't people accuse doctors that they spread diseases? The logic is exactly the same. However, the profession of the physician is a very old and long-established one and the ethical principles there are well known. People have learned to

trust the members of this profession. But this is a millennia-old profession. Compared to that, our profession is very new.

Many antivirus professionals stated that they were continually asked by the general public about their role in generating computer viruses as a form of job security. The service discourse is continually questioned, challenged, and subverted by the dominant understanding of a market economy. The antivirus industry is smeared by the taint of its profit orientation. The authoritative pronouncements of altruistic service are stripped of reverence and admiration. Lamenting the respect accorded physicians, this researcher both questions and concedes the suspicions attached to the industry's service ideals. The profit model of the antivirus industry renders it merely another player in the security market, reliant solely on its capacity to deliver a competitive product, and doubted because of that reliance.

Scanners

Thus, there is an unsolved skepticism when profit is seen as the highest value of the antivirus industry. This skepticism is reinforced when there is also a simultaneous increase in the rapid spread of malware attacks. Profiting within information capitalism leads to a questioning of the actual motivations, strategies, and technologies for protecting the flow of information. From this perspective, the antivirus technology itself is doubted.

Indeed, people scrutinize the antivirus industry's monolithic and uniform use of scanners as 'the' solution to malware. At its most basic level, a scanner looks through files or messages coming into a network. It searches for patterns or 'strings' that exhibit qualities of malware already seen and studied. If a 'scan string' (also known as a 'signature') is found, the suspect file or message is 'quarantined' or blocked. Files suspected of being new malware are sent to the antivirus vendor to be checked for viruses, Trojans, spyware, or other malicious code. After analyzing these files, the vendor revises their scan string, or signature, database. These revisions are distributed as updates so that detection and protection is potentially always current and comprehensive. Most antivirus solutions require users to subscribe for an annual fee. In return, users get to regularly download scan string updates, allowing their scanner to identify the latest malicious code.

This type of scanning is the model of malware protection used by corporations. According to *Wired News* (Delio 2004), in 2003, the Department of Trade and Industry in the United Kingdom established that 93 percent of small businesses and 99 percent of large companies utilized virus scanner software. The study also suggested that close to 60 percent of these businesses automatically update their antivirus software. And it is the same for the home user. A *Consumer Reports* article cited in *The Washington Post* stated that from 2003 to 2005 home users invested more than $2.6 billion on scanning-based software to protect their computers (Krebs 2005).

However, according to the United Kingdom study, in 2003 computer viruses still managed to hit 50 percent of the smaller businesses and infect 68 percent of the larger companies' networks. And according to *The Washington Post* article, from 2003 to 2005 United States consumers spent $9 million for computer repairs and parts due to damage caused by viruses and malware.

It is these kinds of statistics that generate questions about the motivation and strategies of the entire antivirus industry. With a revenue of $4 billion worldwide in 2005 ("Big Bucks," *Virus Bulletin* 2006), the industry's success is attributed to supplying relatively ineffectual protection that keeps customers continually dependent upon—some say 'addicted to'—limited updates for protection. The industry is seen as content with perpetuating a technology that is profitable for their companies, but problematic for the user. The real-world ineffectiveness of scanning is identified by *The Washington Post* author as the antivirus industry's "dirty little secret."

> For example, the dirty little secret of the antivirus industry has always been that because the software generally relies on 'signatures', or snippets of known viruses in order to detect them, each time there's a big new virus outbreak about 10 percent of the industry's customers invariably serve as the guinea pigs for the rest of them. This shortcoming is especially dangerous given the increase in targeted attacks against corporations here and abroad.
> (Krebs 2005)

This articulation of the 'dirty little secret' runs counter to much of the service ideal continually voiced by antivirus professionals. The 'dirty little secret' identifies protection and 'immunity' coming from the first 'guinea pigs' who succumb to an unknown, yet-to-be-identified piece of malicious code. Yet those 'guinea pigs' are still paying for protection, paying the same price for immunity, and may in fact be the target of an attack. All customers are vulnerable to being part of that 'first 10 percent' that must be 'sacrificed' in order for the scan string to be documented. Within this 'protection through infection' model, a certain number of customers must be infected before an 'antidote' is manufactured.

Development of an alternative to the scanning–immunity model is cited as unfairly restricted. Indeed, the lack of technological innovation beyond scanners is charged to the antivirus industry's profit motivation. According to *Wired News* (Delio 2004):

"What you have now is antivirus technology that has been fossilizing for years," said George Smith, a senior fellow with GlobalSecurity.org. "All technologies outside of signature-based scanning were effectively driven from the market in the last decade, as far as the average person or company is concerned. This was a conscious war prosecuted by the market leaders, who have enforced a stagnant technology base. Antivirus technology development is now a radioactive no-man's land."

In the same article, another source is quoted:

"The signature model is totally outdated and virtually useless," said Mike Sweeney, owner of the network-security consulting firm Packetattack, and author of several books on systems security for technology professionals. "But bottom line: Signature files are profitable. You have to have a subscription that they charge either a monthly fee for or an up-front, once-a-year fee. That makes for a nice tidy revenue stream."

Other technological options are described as overlooked and disregarded because the subscription charged for antivirus scanning, either monthly or an up-front, then once-a-year fee, is profitable for the antivirus company. The 'addictive update model', as it has been labeled (Rosenberger 2004), creates a revenue stream that is seen as inhibiting alternative innovations. 'Addictive updates' create frequent and visible alerts that generate corporate customers dependent upon and eager to pay for the protection service.[1]

Some corporate end users commented upon the effectiveness of scanning. While many of them suggest their antivirus vendors were updating frequently and did have a good detection rate for new viruses, several also matter-of-factly identified scanners as allowing some viruses inside their networks.

> CORPORATE END USER STEVEN: If you think back to the case of macro viruses, nobody was scanning for that sort of stuff then because it wasn't considered a threat. So, they had to rewrite their whole product to include being able to scan for this entirely new sort of thing.

> CORPORATE END USER KENNETH: We had a look through and it turned out that our e-mail scanners only scanned the attachments and not the body of messages. So, Kak Worm goes in the sender's signatures in the message body, so you don't even see it on the e-mail scanner. So we've actually probably got a fair infection of Kak Worm, but it was impossible to tell.

As exemplified in the quotes above, the corporate end users neither berate their vendors for bungling the protection of their network, nor do they suggest alternatives. No one questioned their scanner's technological proficiency. These corporate end users seemed to take it for granted that scanners are the best, perhaps even only, option. A vendor comments about the relationship between corporate end users and scanners:

---

[1] It is not my intent to explore the technological rationales for or against scanning technology, or alternatives such as integrity checking or heuristic scanners. My objective is to analyze the antivirus industry discourses surrounding technological innovation and, specifically in this chapter, how the industry articulates and negotiates the seeming contradictions between their service ideals and the compromises of working within a capitalistic economic system.

VENDOR TIMOTHY: The AV companies get to decide what products are available. We don't know anything other than
scanners. When you get right down to it, you have to tell
the customer what's going on. And the best way to do that
is with a scanner. But there's not many options available.
So, I know, it's capitalism in action.

Scanners are the best way to inform customers, to make the actions conducted by the antivirus software visible to the customer.
Scanners display, for the customer, physical evidence that the antivirus
software is processing data. It is not suggested that scanners are necessarily the best vehicle for protection. It is 'capitalism in action'.

Indeed, 'capitalism in action' is held responsible for the scanners
as 'the' type of antivirus technology that is currently available. 'Capitalism in action' is also responsible for the lack of other options. 'Capitalism' becomes the point of reference used to justify the range of
technological decisions and eliminates any individual or collective responsibility for the strategic lack of technological innovation. Indeed,
antivirus companies are the innovators. They decide what technologies
are packaged into the products made available for their customers.
Customers here are seen as passive, as only able to purchase what the
vendors conceptualize as profitable technological solutions.

The industry is charged with remaining stagnant and unchanging,
locked in time unless prodded by a profitable rationale to change. A researcher passionately comments on industry transformations and the
lack of impetus for technological change:

RESEARCHER KEITH: It changes because of market pressure.
That's why I presented a paper [about scanners]. I was trying to tell the corporate people about if they wanted something fundamentally better than scanning. Because the
industry itself by and large, is reactive. They react to criticism and they slowly change as a result of pressure from
the customer base. The industry isn't going to turn around
and say, "Look, actually, this whole scanning paradigm is
shit. It was from the day we started. We knew that. We told
you these are the downsides." But they were countered by
various aspects of the computing environment. And so at

the time we went, "Okay, well, there are the good things and the bad things, and okay, that sort of balances up." Well, all the bad things have got a lot worse and the good things have got worse, so it's now like way out of kilter like this [gestures]. Which says we have to do something else. But they are never going to do that. The only way they are going to change what they do, is if the people who write the checks every year say, "No, that's crap. We want something that does this." And that's only going to happen if the people that write the checks know what to say. Because by and large they don't. They've got this tradition of buying antivirus that is scanning-based antivirus software.

I: So who's responsibility then is it to get these check-writing people to change?

RESEARCHER KEITH: Mine? [laughs] There seems to be significant spokespeople, or they seem to have a significant voice within the AVIEN group. And they are starting to say things that to my ears are more in line with my way of thinking about the best way to make things better is to ditch scanning and get a different model. Because the things that used to make some of the other alternatives poor choices in the distant past, now are much more in the users' way of making those types of approaches, not just plausible, but definitely doable, viable.

According to this researcher, the antivirus industry could move away from the scanner to an alternative model to a more proactive and preventative virus protection strategy. Technological change has transformed the pros and cons of scanning, tilting the balance away from scanners as the limited bastion of antivirus security. Yet the industry has not changed. It remains immobile, the industry unable or unwilling to adapt to other technological innovations.

Responsibility for this lack of antivirus technological innovation is given to the market. Economic pressure from corporate customers, those who 'write the checks', is required to spur technological innovation. Yet these corporate customers are framed as docile, as eager consumers complicit in their own subordination to their vendor's profit orientation, needing a researcher to raise them out of the established paradigm. Through their dependency, through their 'addiction' to the update model, they have been neutralized, accepting the model already present in the wider network. They are voiceless, undemanding, merely using the technology 'given' to them. Through customer groups like AVIEN, some noise is beginning to be made about 'ditching scanning'. The industry, however, is portrayed as locked and trapped by market forces, powerless to move forward and to innovate beyond scanners. A corporate end user states:

> CORPORATE END USER EDWARD: We don't . . . we could pre-protect from a lot of these viruses. But, I mean . . . from a business sense, if there is no money in doing it, then why do it, right? Supply and demand, right? And that's, you know, if you're coming from a business, you have to understand the AV industry.

Scanners and capitalism perform conjointly, producing a set of relationships in which both seem enduring and unalterable. The market and money are the dominant forces guiding technological development. Money and the market are fundamental to organizing both the ideals and practices within the antivirus industry. By defining and structuring the relation between threats and security, and prescribing scanners as the only technology to cope with malicious code, money and the market are seen as the influential industry powers. Service ideals become hollow echoes.

This combined force of technological and economic determinism is seen as curtailing both innovation and the arrival of 'new blood' or inventive ideas into the industry.

> VENDOR TIMOTHY: You cannot get a new company into this field now. I would be amazed to see a new company come into this field. Because you have to go back through these 50,000 viruses and detect them. Because the whole thing is predicated on detecting these 50,000 things that no one ever, ever sees, apart from in 'zoos'. You couldn't do it. The manpower expenditure would be amazing. It's hard enough just to keep up. But to have to process a backlog of 50,000? So, it's those people who have been in the industry

for a long time can stay there because they can keep up, maybe they can go faster and faster and faster perhaps, but they can keep up. They can do that because they've more and more money. But you can't start in this field now. As an individual you can, although that's also pretty difficult. But as a company, I don't think so. I don't think there's ever going to be a new scanner.

The 'manpower expenditure' is seen as leading to the closing of innovation and the free flow of new ideas and technologies into the industry. A new type of scanner, or a revolutionary technology, is blocked by the inability to process all past viruses and the financial resources to support that process. These financial pressures inhibit new technological growth and development, making it impossible for new innovators to enter the industry. In this sense, the scanner is technologically fixed and permanent, and an expression of the logic and coercions of advanced capitalism (Orlikowski 2000). Technology and capitalism interact and determine each other, influencing and reflecting the various technological, moral, and commercial interests of the industry in a technologically stagnant yet ever-expanding cycle of profit generation.

Marketing

The antivirus industry is indeed a growing commercial enterprise. According to *Virus Bulletin*, antivirus software revenues reached $4 billion worldwide in 2005, an increase of 13.6 percent over the previous year.[2] However, many of the marketing tactics used to achieve that success are critiqued. Indeed, strategies used by vendors to promote their unique solutions for countering malicious code, and thus their superiority over other vendors, conflict with industry ideals of protecting and servicing the security of network communication.

---

[2] Industry analyst Gartner reported that enterprise and consumer sales accounted for 51.5 percent and 48.5 percent of revenues, respectively ("Big Bucks," *Virus Bulletin* 2006). Microsoft, seen as the epitome of profit orientation, was beginning to enter the antivirus market toward the end of the interviews but at that time was specifically focused on the home user and was not considered by many in the industry to be a real threat to the corporate customers' dollars.

Specifically critiqued is the promotion of a portending technological apocalypse. Vendors are accused of raising fears of an outbreak in order to sell their products as the solution. Their unique antivirus products are represented as able to protect against and reverse this catastrophe. In an endless angst-ridden cycle, many vendors incite this kind of worry and anxiety in end users, and then attempt to relieve these emotions through promotion of their antivirus software.

> VENDOR GARY: Lots of people make comments and accuse us many, many times of the fact that our marketing team is out of control, and our PR team is out of control, and we put press releases out, okay? What they don't know is, I actually have the final word before a press release goes out the door. And the only one that can override me in a press release is the president of the company. So, you know, we've gone to great lengths over the past couple of years in taking the people that were with the group, and there's only a couple of them, and we've rebuilt the entire organization and bought this other company to make sure that we walk this fine line between promoting the company, promoting the work that we do, and staying as true to the roots that the AV community has set up, so that we. . . . And we think that we've been extremely successful by it. But we know that there is still this cloud that hangs over our head because of the big bad, you know, capitalistic, number one, you know, Americana thing that we have going for ourselves.

The contradictions, the tensions, and the negotiations inherent within the industry are amplified as each antivirus marketing representative attempts to promote his vendor's service and its products. Negotiating the conflicting demands is articulated as 'walking a fine line' between upholding the service 'roots' of the antivirus community and promoting the specific antivirus company. This vendor has gone to 'great lengths', and the company has been 'rebuilt' to accommodate those 'roots'. However, he acknowledges that the 'big, bad capitalist Americana' cloud remains linked with their past promotional strategies. His company, its marketing team, its public relations team, and its press releases were stigmatized as 'out of control'. According to this vendor, promoting the company and drawing upon the 'number one Americana thing' is a fraught enterprise as vendors must straddle contradictory mandates inherent in both the industry's service roots and a techno-capitalist economy.

The tensions between 'big bad capitalism' and the antivirus industry's 'roots' of cooperation and sharing are repeatedly negotiated in the global marketplace. Marketing departments must differentiate their own antivirus products from those of other vendors. In antivirus marketing perspective, the vendor that is first to recognize the beginning of a virus outbreak and discover a unique solution to the epidemic is 'first to market'. Being 'first to market' earns a strategic marketing opportunity. It allows the demonstration and promotion of that vendor's competence and superiority over its slower, less effective, less responsive competitors. In this sense, each virus outbreak becomes a propitious circumstance for a vendor's self-promotion. However, the service roots of antivirus decree that new virus samples are shared cooperatively between researchers so that the entire global networked community can be protected. Service roots conflict with gaining an advantage in the competitive global marketplace. Below, a vendor articulates his thought processes in a conversation he had with a researcher who objected to both his marketing strategy and his proprietary attitude toward his company's discovery of a new computer virus. Instead of providing a sample to other researchers and thus allowing all antivirus vendors to quickly produce detection updates and prevent a potential world-wide network catastrophe, this vendor supplied a sample to the rest of the industry only several days after his company had released information to the media. He promoted the new virus' potential destructiveness and mobility and his company's unique solution. This vendor recalls his confrontation with a service-oriented researcher:

> VENDOR GARY: We have this virus. I said to him, "I told you I would give you something when I could give it to you. I made a promise. I wasn't going to break my promise," I said. My hands were simply tied. I said, "Now frankly, this is a business." And I said, "We're in a capitalistic society from where I graduated from and know from. I could have said, 'Fuck everybody!' and buried you all and gave you nothing.

And that would have just been the way that it was." So, I
said, "But you know, I got you where you needed to get to."
I said, "In the future, I'll do what I need to do, and then get
you what I need to get."

This vendor issued a media alert about the virus, was the 'first to
market', and decided to keep the virus exclusively within his own company, hyping their discovery and solutions before releasing it for other
vendors to analyze. Within his conceptualization, the virus became his
'property', and gave him the ability to do 'what he needed to do' as defined within market logic. He is the 'owner' of the virus, and through his
rights of ownership, he has the ability to develop his market identity at
the expense of the excluded others, the 'non-owners' (Wark 2004). He
justifiably establishes and enforces a relationship of scarcity around his
possession. He prioritizes the opportunity to market his own company's
competitive edge within a capitalistic economy. "This is a business."

For this vendor, company profits and marketing profiles were evaluated as more important than the communal 'roots' dedicated to
protecting information flows. Instead of envisioning a worldwide interdependent information society, instead of protecting the entire networked communication infrastructure, and instead of prioritizing his
responsibility to assure maximum global detectablity for that structure,
he kept the virus from everyone outside his company until several days
after he had made a promotional press release and had given several
high-profile media interviews. Living within techno-capitalism and applying his graduate school business education, he presents his decision
to exclude the rest of the industry as realistic and sound.

Since all antivirus vendors must similarly labor to detect, analyze,
and efficiently apply solutions to malware, the source of productivity
and growth lies in that company's ability to uniquely manipulate and
more quickly apply technological solutions to circulated virus samples.
Promotion of that capability and speed become an important practice
through which vendors display their distinctiveness and superiority.
Information and knowledge about these samples are then decisive
tools in generating profits and in appropriating market shares (Wark
2004). From this perspective, the vendor's decision above is rational
and justifiable. Virus samples are a category of economic utility in his
business pursuit.

The vendor above presents this market logic of antivirus as a neutral inevitability, as a form of economic realism within which he must operate. In fact, he states his "hands are tied." "This is business" is used to justify closing off information from others, his timing and his strategic choices in effect remove him from personal responsibility for the safety of the net. However, by defining and structuring the relationship between vendors and prescribing his own 'rationale' as the only professional, business way to conceptualize these relationships, he establishes himself and his educational background as the evaluator of the necessary timing and sharing of information. For this vendor, controlling the release of virus samples generates the potential for his and his company's ability to dominate and succeed within the industry.

The contradictions inherent in the discourse of service and this discourse of marketing and profit generate contrasting identities and social positions within the industry. Vendors as 'marketroids' and 'salesdroids', as one corporate end user labeled them, are contrasted with the tireless researcher or well-informed and overworked technician. The vendor quoted above recognizes his occupational status as the 'marketroid' of his company:

VENDOR GARY: I'm in a sense probably somewhat controversial, you know, because if you get into the hard core technical side of it and the research side of it, there shouldn't be all this hype and this, all this marketing stuff that goes around it, right? But that's part of my job. And there's also a little bit of a stigma that goes on with me. I'm the person that when we have a situation like a virus outbreak or our company decides that it's our responsibility to let customers know about something that people have been talking about, I'm that person.

This vendor acknowledges his place within the industry. He knows he is controversial and stigmatized. When compared to the researcher or the 'hard core technical side', his job is merely 'hyping' and 'marketing stuff'. Yet he also states it is his responsibility to inform customers and to articulate his company's position on a virus outbreak. Through marketing techniques, through industry positioning, and through image creation, his job is to update, influence, and shape impressions of his company.

This type of commercialization and marketing by vendors is a source of continual conflict within the industry. Basic marketing tactics used by 'marketroids' to inform about new crises and their company's superior solutions are seen to highlight vendor profit over industry service, and money over security. Marketing plays a crucial, albeit paradoxical, role in this articulation of the antivirus industry's identity.

Disciplining Marketing

As suggested by the vendor above, in the continual negotiations and power plays between the marketing and the service ideals, the stigmatized 'marketroids' learn to accommodate and work within antivirus industry 'roots', boundaries, and ideals. And even though the researcher Michael, cited at the beginning of this chapter, suggests that "money always has control," this same researcher also suggests that researchers have the power and authority to collectively influence industry directions. Researchers, as industry veterans, enforce disciplining procedures on those vendor marketing and PR departments that do not comply. When discussing these methods, he describes the techniques:

> RESEARCHER MICHAEL: The more veteran of the group will generally lead by way of showing them how to interact with each other. And we have, on occasion, the more veteran of the group, forced certain other company PR teams into line by subjecting them to isolation or sanctions in some way.
>
> I: And where does this happen?
>
> RESEARCHER MICHAEL: Behind the scenes. Primarily in e-mail.
>
> I: Are we talking CARO? Who's doing this?
>
> RESEARCHER MICHAEL: No, not just. CARO is the oldest of these groups, but there are other groups now. With each group of people, they recognize that this is the way the industry does things and through that communication, you share information. And you, you, do not force upon others,

but you make everyone recognize that the proper thing to
do is to share the technical information. Scientific fact is
not to be held. And if you don't play by those rules, then
people will frown upon you.

To be a member of the antivirus industry, one must abide by the
formal and informal rules of the 'community' or face isolation and exclusion. This researcher counsels that scientific and technical information is to be shared. This expectation and the corresponding sanctions
for failure to comply are applied even to the marketing and PR departments. Resources and knowledges cannot be exploited or kept for a
vendor's own exclusive benefit. Individuals are not 'forced', but 'come
to recognize' the shared benefit of advancing technological information and scientific fact.

One cornerstone of industry identity is the open communication
of scientific fact and the progress that results from networked collaboration. Without this openness, mutual shared communication would
stall, hampering the productivity of those collaborative efforts. As this
researcher suggests, "scientific fact is not to be held." This position is
similar to the basic rule of scholarly research and development in
which all findings must be open and communicated in a form that allows peer review and criticism. Drawing on the academic ideals inherent in the mythical birth of the internet, this researcher's justification
for disciplining wayward industry professionals is rooted in the scholarly tradition of the shared pursuit of science, peer review, and openness in all research findings.

Confronting wayward vendors entails sometimes challenging their
business strategies 'behind the scenes'. At other times, confronting
wayward vendors means threatening them or creating crises for them.
Whether indirect or direct confrontation, strategic alliances are generated by technology researchers against 'marketing people'. CARO-like
groups intervene in the process of the vendor's marketing strategies
with the goal of achieving compliance. They attempt to foster a cultural and political hegemony within the industry that all understand
and voluntarily accommodate. CARO-like groups use their power to
support, reinforce, and influence the status of other technical managers over and above 'marketing people'.

RESEARCHER CHARLES: We sometimes create crises for other organizations. We don't like doing that. And we certainly don't regard that as giving us power. But sometimes it does. Sometimes we will very specifically do it if we see a technical manager being overridden by marketing people. Sometimes it's absolutely essential.

Creating a crisis for organizations that have been overrun by 'marketing people' is seen as essential. Through this collective pressure, technical managers are elevated as knowledgeable and connected experts. Wayward marketing strategists come to 'recognize' their need for and respect of information capital and the technology experts who create and share it. Disciplining 'marketroids' through creating 'crises' results in changed attitudes and voluntary compliance. One researcher comments upon a wayward, relatively new antivirus company and its struggle for a share of the American market:

RESEARCHER KEITH: What these people say is, "Ah, but we are [Company Name] in [Country]. The guys that did that are in the U.S. We don't have any control over our United States distributor." This is the sort of bullshit excuses that people were using eight years ago, that everyone accepts now are bullshit. Okay, they are your distributor. That means you are supplying them product. That means you have the ultimate lever to control the way they behave. You stop supplying them product. And if you are not prepared to do that, that means that you aren't serious about the way your product is perceived, the way that it is marketed. They say, "Oh no, but we couldn't do that because we've got contracts and things." And you say, "Ah, but if you didn't put a clause in your contract that allows that kind of control over the perception of your product, then you don't care about how your product is seen. And so how do you expect us to trust you?"

Antivirus vendors that fail to harmonize their actions and marketing orientations with the ethical 'roots' of the rest of the industry are seen as refusing to comply with sanctioned rules and procedures.

They are seen as untrustworthy and are excluded and isolated accordingly.

Antivirus marketing is done in a kind of 'glass house' with all aspects of the vendor's rationales and strategies visible for critique and sanction. All antivirus companies are expected to have the approved and consistent marketing strategy across all international markets. This approved market strategy is suggested to be more important than business contracts. Suppliers must discipline their distributors into complying with industry marketing standards or be punished, disciplined, or isolated for noncompliance.

Significantly, the 'market' is not portrayed as 'out there', completely beyond human hands or behaviors of the antivirus marketing professional (Cheney 1998). These industry professionals do not allow such a reification of 'the market'. As articulated in the vendor quote above, researchers as a power block of technological experts do not allow the market to be removed from the influence of the individual 'marketroid'. Instead, the 'marketroid' is held accountable to alter an exploitive and irresponsible system.

The result is a 'voluntary' upholding and embracing of these collaborative ideals. Through panoptic surveillance, through the exclusion and removal of those who do not comply, discipline is maintained. This forced sharing and collaboration then comes to form the identity architecture of the industry. There are no specific governmental policies or laws governing the industry. Instead, isolation is an effective form of regulation and discipline of individual behaviors. Technological isolation affects the bottom line and also affects that vendor's market position.

And it works. Another vendor comments on the effect of 'industry influence':

VENDOR BRIAN: There are well-defined rules of the industry and there are well-defined communications within the members of the industry. There are self-regulatory bodies. There are industry publications which are old and mature, okay? And there is a thing which I would call industry influence. When some industry members do the wrong things, if enough other members say, "No, no, no, you can't do it!" it is very likely the company at fault would back off immediately.

Well-defined rules and communications, and self-regulatory bodies and industry publications all generate what this vendor identifies as 'industry influence'. Industry influence produces compliance among industry players so that all facets of the industry, from the CEO to 'marketroids', conform in definitions of threats, security, marketing strategies, and the needs of their customers.

One vendor discusses his 'conversion' after a discussion with an influential researcher. The vendor is not 'forced' but comes to 'recognize' how, if he wanted to stay within the industry and succeed, he needed to change his marketing orientation and strategy to better conform to the antivirus industry's unique standards.

> VENDOR GARY: Ultimately [the researcher] just simply said that while he understands the business side of things and where I'm coming from, basically this won't work in this industry because of the way the industry works. And the fact that if I was going to succeed or wanted to stay in the industry, that I had to, you know, operate within the same context that was already set up in the industry or I'd be screwed. Because if I don't give everybody a sample so they can protect their customers, my customers are going to end up being bombarded by the infections that people send to them, even though they can protect it. It's just a pain. You can't do business that way and so, that just doesn't work.

This vendor was told in no uncertain terms that if he wanted to succeed, he needed to "operate within the same context that was already set up in the industry." If he did not want to "be screwed," he had to adjust his marketing techniques to the industry networking standards already in place. This vendor comes to see that his own corporate customers, even though they are protected by his company's new antidote, could be bombarded by other unprotected systems. Not independent or isolated, the worldwide networked integration becomes a 'pain' for the globalized customers he is paid to protect. He 'recognizes' that within the antivirus industry, 'you can't do business that way'. He articulates and now promotes sharing information with everyone as a viable business model.

While focusing on the service and protection he provides his customers, this vendor articulates his conversion to these industry norms. He has become complicit and compliant, articulating his personal attitude change. The expert researcher, has opened the door, has shown him the industry-wide rationale for 'doing business'. There is indeed a common cultural code in the diverse workings of the antivirus companies and their various industry sectors. Though the industry is comprised of many vocational orientations, values, and projects that cross through and inform the strategies of the various professionals in the industry, they discipline newcomers into the one industry ideal of sharing, trust, and service as the rationale of business logic.

The sharing–trust–service ideal forges links between marketing and the technological systems. These links are a form of regulation and discipline that integrate the market with ethical and service norms. However, this sharing–trust–service orientation does not become a condemnation of contemporary techno-capitalism. The sharing–trust–service ideal does not turn into a radical critique for the transformation of the industry's social, cultural, economic, or technological arrangements. Instead, sharing, trust, and service become merely the enforced business model of the industry, an effective way of protecting corporate money within a market economy. It becomes the antivirus way of 'doing business'.

Media

The foundational paradox of the antivirus industry—both providing the service for securing the internet, while simultaneously assuring profits for antivirus companies—is also magnified in the industry's dealing with the media. Indeed, the mass media plays a significant role in the processes involved in building the antivirus industry's identity, in many ways creating, ritualizing, and disseminating information to the general public, other computer specialists, and their corporate customers. Exploiting scare tactics through unnecessary and dramatic press releases about computer virus infections had its heyday at the turn of the century, though it still continues. There was and still is media hype about the advent of IT-based 'super viruses'. This formulaic narrative is evident in the following selective sampling of prominent news organizations' headlines: "Flaw in Microsoft Word Used in Computer Attack" (*The New York Times* 2006), "Virtually Unprotected: An Insecure Nation" (*The New York Times* 2005), "Worm Brings Down PCs and Networks" (*The New York Times* 2004), "New Computer Virus Circles Globe" (*The Wall Street Journal* 2003), "Cyberspace Invaders" (*Consumer Reports* 2002), "The Doomsday Click" (*The New Yorker* 2001), and "Love Bug Virus Creates Worldwide Chaos" (*The Guardian* 2000). Stressing the 'world-killing' danger in representations of destruction, 'cyber-tsunamis', or 'electronic Pearl Harbors', the media report worst-case scenarios with suggestions that the internet and nation-states are being brought to their knees.

Journalists tracking the effects of computer virus epidemics contact corporate end users, researchers, and vendor marketing departments when a virus outbreak occurs in order to document the destruction inherent in narratives of 'technology out of control'. Both corporate end users and researchers see this contact as exploitive and slanted.

> CORPORATE END USER EDWARD: When the last virus came out, *The New York Times* called me, all kinds of other publications called me to see how much damage was done, you know. That's all they want to do is sensationalize everything and see how much damage was done, you know, but yeah. There's a lot of problems with the media.

> RESEARCHER WILLIAM: Ah, every time I'm in the U.S. I'm interviewed by journalists for newspapers and they all ask the same questions about how terrible the internet has gotten, and how much worse they think, how much worse it still can get. Basically what they decide is the concept of *Terminator 3*—machines take over. Response times, people want faster response times. They are going to use software to find malicious software, so computers are going to fight computers.

The media is negated for sensationalizing seemingly unsubstantiated big threats. It is seen as exaggerating and focusing exclusively on damages and destruction, and hyping ruptures to informational infrastructures to the point of creating science fiction.

The news audience is also implicated in the sensationalization of technological destruction. Reporters are seen as both responding to and influencing the uninformed and scared news consumers, so that narratives about ominous technology overshadow an accurate report about technological facts. A corporate end user describes his perspective of the connection between journalists and their audiences:

> CORPORATE END USER STEVEN: Most of them don't understand the issues, but that is true of the media in general, and what their audience wants. Most 'news consumers' are no more interested in an accurate, complete report on a virus than they are with in-depth reporting of, oh, anything. There are a few reporters who want to get it right, but most news is interest-driven, that is to say, "Can we make it look scary and important?" not "Is this really newsworthy?" A lot of the real antivirus stuff isn't interesting to the general public. "Antivirus software stops most viruses more than four months before it gets a foothold in the wild!" isn't a headline that will sell papers. But research showed that it was true. "New Virus Attacks Blondes; No Cure Known!" is an entirely different issue. *That* will move some copy!

This corporate end user suggests that the headline hype about "New Virus Attacks Blondes; No Cure Known" will stimulate purchases, that news consumers are interested in narratives about computer viruses only as an invasive force that continually threatens to attack targeted, uninformed victims. He does not see journalists as understanding viruses, nor interested in the real significance of virus threats. They are seen as merely providing fear-provoking copy for frightened news consumers. Indeed, journalists highlight fear of attacks, fear of being controlled by technology, and fear of being unable to control the ultimate direction of technological change.

Antivirus professionals then hold journalists responsible for constructing these narratives. Through this process of confronting mediated stories about computer viruses, these antivirus professionals become critical media theorists themselves. They continually articulated oppositional positions against the media's taken-for-granted assumptions and its unsupported 'facts'. Their critique expands from the media's specific representation of computer viruses to generalized mediated constructions of 'true' and 'correct' information.

RESEARCHER DANIEL: The specialty of journalists is to write stories. The problem is that they have to write about so many subjects, there is no way they can be experts in all those subjects. What they really know how to do is how to write stories. They don't know how to find out what is true and what is correct. So basically about any subject they write, they don't know what the premise is. And it's not just about antiviruses. It's about anything.

Journalists construct narratives, not disseminate what this researcher suggests is 'true' and 'correct' information. Antivirus professionals continually confront the narrative aspect of 'news' as they attempt to counter the sensationalized portrayal of outbreaks. Through this confrontation, they contest the basic motivations and assumptions guiding journalistic reports 'about anything'.

When, then, should an antivirus professional discuss a potential virus outbreak with a reporter? At what point does a virus become 'newsworthy'? Releasing a virus alert to the press is always problematic. Informing the media about a new computer virus is the epitome of the service-profit double-bind confronted by all antivirus vendors. As a service to the internet community, everyone should know when a virus epidemic is imminent. Yet, predicting the point of an outbreak is difficult and fraught with public relations issues. One vendor comments:

VENDOR TIMOTHY: One of the problems is that it's hard to predict how well a virus will spread. If you, as an AV company, find a couple of instances of a certain virus in the wild, how are you to determine if that virus is about to burn down the net, or never be seen again? You can make educated guesses based on the properties of the virus, where it was found, how it got there, things like that. But if you go public and say, "Everyone must watch out for this deadly new virus" and then it doesn't happen, you look like a scaremonger. If it does happen, you look like Nostradamus, and you've done your customers a service. If you don't go public, and it burns down the net, then you go public later, you look like you're jumping on the bandwagon. Tricky stuff.

Releasing an alert to the press about a virus outbreak can be both a service that warns people to protect their networks, and simultaneously, a marketing strategy. The definition depends on the end result of the outbreak. When a vendor releases an alert, that alert both enacts a service ideal, while at the same time promotes its superior software. The duality of the seemingly oppositional ethical quandary between using the media to provide a service or merely promoting a software product is resolved through alerts that are accurate and focused, which is in itself a complex and politically volatile determination.

Much of the antivirus industry sees itself as having a responsibility not to contribute to media 'scaremongering' and exaggeration. It was continually stated, even by the PR marketing representatives, that the service orientation should outweigh both the need to generate media interest and the strategic development of brand recognition.

> VENDOR TIMOTHY: Historically, the media likes viruses. More specifically, it likes viruses that emerge out of nowhere all of a sudden, and infect the world before anyone's ready to deal with them. Like all things mass-market-media-related, it's not news unless it's exciting. News media doesn't report, "Small fire in chip pan, put out in two minutes by local volunteer fire brigade." They will instead report, "Huge fire burns out six city blocks, where was local volunteer fire brigade?" The fact that the brigade was out at the chip pan fire that would have burnt out seven city blocks had they not been there, is not interesting to the media. And that's fine. Not a problem. It's the responsibility of AV companies not to make a mountain out of a molehill, not to puff up the importance of a virus just to garner media interest and name recognition.

While antivirus professionals negate the media's exaggeration of anxiety-producing coverage and its lack of in-depth reporting, antivirus companies are seen to have an obligation not to exploit these media narratives for their own advantage. Brand identity and marketing should not be the goal. Vendors' responsibilities entail not contributing to media reports that overstate the effects of suddenly emerging and potentially dangerous virus threats merely to promote their company's image and software.

However, while this responsibility is articulated, many antivirus professionals cite the relationship between vendors' marketing departments and the media as an exploitive collaboration garnered to do just that—sell each vendor's image and products. It was continually suggested that antivirus marketing departments feed worst-case scenarios to journalists. This is considered an ill-fated alliance because neither 'marketroids' nor journalists are equipped to accurately convey the significance of virus threats, yet they both strategically exploit each other to advance their own products and objectives.

Together, reporters and antivirus marketing representatives are perceived as complexly entwined within a consumer economy. Reporters and marketing representatives jointly promote the fears at the heart of 'news consumers' in a techno-capitalist society so that selling stories and selling software are conflated. Fear of technology is subsumed to the requirements of the highly abstract and impersonal objectives of late capitalism. Media are not considered independent sources of knowledge used to inform an apprehensive public, but instead are seen as too quickly 'jumping on' stories, and with the help of antivirus marketing, promoting fear and calamity.

Most antivirus vendors, however, do not see themselves as merely focused on making money and increasing the recognition and industry rating of their specific company. They too are immersed within and uphold the industry 'roots', attempting to provide a genuine service to the information society. Nevertheless, they are accountable to their stakeholders for the profit margin of their software and for their company's ranking in the computer security sector. Consequently, their work must straddle the oppositional orientations of service and of marketing. They attempt to control the mass media within the bounds of industry perimeters. When asked if there were other issues I should cover in my interviews with antivirus professionals, one representative of a large antivirus vendor articulated the vendors' perspective of both sides of this service–marketing media dilemma. In answering the question, he reveals the tension and strain inherent in his responsibility of dealing with the media, and simultaneously straddling the paradox of a service industry's orientation within a capitalistic economy:

VENDOR BRIAN: You should be asking questions about the role
of the media. You should be asking questions about hyping. You should be asking questions about the bad tactics
of scaring people with stupid press releases, which I have
to tell you my company was never guilty of. Because people would say that we have been doing that. And I tell you,
every single time, I would proof the press release that
would be going out. And in my technological opinion, this
press release should go out, okay? Because there is some
particular special area within this particular virus and this
particular threat which I think other people should know,
okay? And some other companies would get upset about it,
especially smaller companies which don't have such a PR
machine like us. But, it is a PR machine which is just part
of our business. We didn't invent it for antivirus only. We
just use our corporate resources, okay?

Through using the media as a marketing resource, this vendor attempts to simultaneously define and stimulate his company's unique
position vis-à-vis the other antivirus companies, while also accommodating the industry's service ethic. He realizes his desire to inform a
particular aspect of the internet community about this particular virus
through the media is seen by some as merely fueling, through fear, the
production of the antivirus commodity. But within this vendor's 'technological opinion', he is justified in releasing information about specific viruses to the press. He is not using 'scare tactics'. Indeed, he
denounces the use of scare tactics. He articulates the antivirus industry's accepted logic and service exemplar that provides information
about threats to the networked society. He is attempting to warn an
admittedly small percentage of that network. In his opinion, he is providing a necessary mediated service. He also identifies how his 'PR
machine' is used by his entire security corporation. Antivirus is merely
one aspect of that business, and in his opinion, he successfully utilizes
this 'corporate resource' for his antivirus product. His actions are justifiable in accordance with both sides of the antivirus industry's service
and marketing agendas. He is, accordingly, not 'hyping' a virus alert.

Antivirus marketing departments and media outlets are given the
power to both reflect and influence public anxiety about the impacts of

the technology, and in that assigned role, are seen as potentially abusing this responsibility by generating unnecessary alerts and unsubstantiated 'hype'. Scaring the public through hype and through gratuitous press releases is always repudiated, even by the vendors themselves, while 'service' is considered as able to predict and precipitously warn the anxious public about the effects of a sudden virus outbreak. The media are complexly integrated with the service and profit links, as vendors straddle the conflict between the need to inform and the profit ideal within information-capitalism.

Conflicting interpretations of who is allowed to send alerts about what kind of threats also swirls around the mediated aspects of cyber terrorism and its consequential reinterpretation of security ideals after 9/11. The antivirus industry's knowledge about cyber terrorism conflicts with many governments' mediated representation of threats. In 2003, a video presentation by Richard Clarke, then the Special Advisor for Cyber Space Security to President George W. Bush, (previously the National Coordinator for Security, Infrastructure Protection, and Counterterrorism on the National Security Council), was shown at various computer security conferences around the world. In this video, Clarke connects terrorism, malicious code, and the 2003 power outages in the Midwest and Eastern United States. Many in the industry condemn these U.S. government definitions, the video, and Clarke himself:

> RESEARCHER KEITH: Richard Clarke, former adviser to the President on cyber terrorism, I'm not sure whether that was actually his official title but it was something like that, had a vested interest in running around and bandying the term 'cyber terrorism' around and dreaming up worst-case scenarios and scaring people, because that basically justified his existence. I think what happened to him is that after September 11, the administration came to realize that, whilst there may be something of a cyber threat, bricks and mortar and large amounts of aviation gas, fire in tall buildings were actually going to get people killed, whereas the 'cyber threat' or the threat of cyber terror were greatly overplayed. So they demoted him and as a result he resigned. But cyber terrorism, yeah, it has been a long-

running joke. There was a long-running healthy disregard for the hype and overstating of the apparent threat as various people in the computer security industry and commentators upon the computer security industry noted and often made fun of Richard Clarke and his cronies.

Richard Clarke, both representing and resigning from the U.S. government, is negated. Clarke is perceived as untrustworthy, promoting misinformation about security. Against attempts to represent himself as 'expert' and therefore best qualified to secure the safety of citizens, many in the antivirus industry counter this stance by warning that he and his cronies' version of terrorism was in fact merely mediated scare tactics and reflective of standard marketing ploys. The antivirus industry is portrayed again as assuming responsibility to counter hyped misinformation, this time about cyber terrorism and a culture of fear.

The antivirus industry's analysis of and railing against the media and government mystification of threat reveals a great deal about the dynamic interplay, contestations, and struggles surrounding its identity as a 'service industry'. In their critical assessments, they expose the hegemonic relations of dominations reflected in the narratives of news reporting. They critique the way politicians, like Richard Clarke, use media to reconfigure political agendas around security. They see the state as either unwilling or unable to restrain computer malware, the conduct of virus writers, and aspects of its own public relations. They accuse the government and the media of being exploiters of social anxieties for their own political agendas. Indeed, many within the industry critique the ideological basis of the popularization of technological insecurities, acknowledging how the government and media disseminate exaggerated, and at times fallacious, claims. Antivirus professionals contest both government's and media's content and strategies, while offering their own political critique. And within their critical assessment of these tactics, they also simultaneously promote their own positions as technology and knowledge experts. While contesting Richard Clarke's and the 'marketroid's' exploitation of threat, they challenge the ground rules of that manipulation, disputing the very basis of the media's knowledge and power generation.

In the process of correcting and challenging media interpretations, many of these antivirus professionals become frustrated with the seeming invisibility of their 'truth', with the lack of interest and unresponsiveness of journalists. Some antivirus professionals continually discussed their attempts to counter the narratives and the scare tactics used by the media:

> RESEARCHER KEITH: I tried for a while to improve things with some of the IT journalists at a couple of large media outlets who actively and often write about virus-related issues. But I don't know, they stopped writing to me asking for my opinions. I'm terribly pedantic and I won't give nice little sound bites like, "It's going to be bigger than LoveLetter," you know. It's not the way I work. And I try to be very factual with these people and if they say something that's not correct, I try to politely and in a clear and as simple way as I can, point out what was wrong with it, why it was misleading, and why it was potentially dangerous. And I guess over a relatively short period of time these people get sick of getting e-mail like this, when all they do is make mistake after mistake after mistake. And they can go to people that are less technical and have a less significant background and have a less informed view of the history of these things and get sound bites. If what you read in the general media about viruses is anything to judge the rest of the general media by, then most of what we hear as news is wrong and often dangerously misleading.

The mediated messages surrounding malware are characterized by a multitude of competing orientations of purpose and content, and thus require continual negotiations and articulations to establish a preferred framing. Industry experts attempt to influence and counteract these mediated efforts by initiating their own contacts with the press, giving specific and detailed information, information they feel is for the most part ignored. The failure to correct the media's 'dangerously misleading' portrayal of computer viruses and to transform knowledge about threats and insecurities results in critiques of the entire mediated news industry. Based on their knowledge of computer virus threats, most within the antivirus industry articulated that much 'news' is fabricated, agenda-driven, and based on false premises. They ultimately question any reality portrayed by news media.

Unable to 'educate' the press, more pressure is placed on transforming the 'marketroid's' orientation toward the media. And it is working. Significantly, since the millennium, many vendors' interactions with the media have been brought under control by their in-house researchers negotiating with their own senior executives. Excessive virus alerts and false statements have been curtailed because any misleading information is seen as having long-term negative consequences affecting the profit margin.

> RESEARCHER KEITH: Some of the large AV companies themselves have taken a more responsible attitude because they have been listening to the views of the senior people within. . . . The research-orientated people are saying, "Look, the bottom line is, this is bad for our image." Okay, yes you get the media publicity in the short term. But in the long term, it damages the image because it makes us look like we are chasing a quick buck. It makes us look like we are trying to make money from other people's misfortune. It makes us look incompetent when a representative of the company goes on the national news and says, "This is going to be bigger than LoveLetter." And then the next day all the major morning newspapers are running stories about how nothing happened, you know, because it is very, very hard to predict.

Mediated scare tactics are seen as damaging both the antivirus industry's reputation and its profit margin. Drawing on 'bottom-line' analogies, this researcher directly connects the short-term media agendas with the long-term repercussions on the industry's profits. "Bigger than LoveLetter" represents technology as out of control, an invasive force that he sees as continually threatening end users' sense of safety on the net, which he suggests those in power come to realize as an unprofitable scaremongering tactic. He suggests that most vendors learn to recognize the damage to their reputation when they are seen as both profiting from end users' misery and anxiety, while also looking incompetent in the face of a technological non-crisis. For the most part, media hype is no longer used as an instrument to drive vendor profit. Marketing departments of the major industry players are no longer blinded by shortsighted capitalistic greed, and largely refrain from colluding with the media.

The fact that there are multiple discourses surrounding both the definition of security and the need to alert the public allows the critiques of commercialization to highlight the differences between legitimate and false alerts, and to sanction disciplinary behavior of those that go to the 'dark side'. The moral high ground of a strong service orientation is contrasted with the excesses of commercialization. By continually ostracizing media and vendor marketing departments, many industry professionals are able to demarcate the boundaries between acceptable and unacceptable behavior, between ethical and corrupt actions. The implementation of the service orientation allows industry professionals to attribute blame within the commercial sector of computer security. In a multimediated world with contesting voices dispersed throughout, this interpretation of 'marketroids' and the media helps to maintain symbolic boundaries of the moral and the immoral within the antivirus industry.

The discourses surrounding the service ideal are translated into strategic decisions and a patchwork of various orientations, experiences, and interests. The service ideal has become a material force that must be negotiated because it informs and enforces powerful economic decisions within the industry. Most antivirus professionals, including the 'marketroids', through their interactions with other industry professionals and through disciplinary actions of exclusion and isolation, come to recognize and voluntarily promote the service ideals. Most antivirus professionals incorporate those ideals into their vision of innovation and productive growth, and into their identities as professionals within the antivirus industry.

Negotiating Marketing and Service

Who determines what is a threat, who should be alerted, and how to communicate knowledge of the threat are all contested arenas within the antivirus industry. Alerting about new virus outbreaks and providing community protection is contrasted with the promotion of individual company agendas, the building of market shares, and the authenticity and reliability of news reporting in general. A press release about the successful detection of a new threat is framed with rules and procedures, grounded within dominant security and service discourses.

However, even with all the negative portrayals of marketing, and even though both marketing and the media are critiqued and maligned by most within the antivirus industry, they are still cultivated as a necessity within the techno-capitalistic economic system. Media and marketing circulate information about antivirus technology and artifacts, and consequently create an environment for demand of a company's products. So, while the industry critiques challenge some aspects of the seemingly corrupting influence of media and marketing power, the industry continues to utilize their combined ability to foster global interest in solutions to malware problems through the purchase of antivirus products.

The antivirus industry discourses are then composed of competing frames of reference and codes of intelligibility. The fact that the spread of malicious code is represented in different and often competing ways has significant implications for the entire industry. In regard to marketing service, it means that there is constant juggling for power and control over both media and the government's representations of threat, as different groups promote their specific agendas. As demonstrated with the negotiation over spam, 9/11, and now scanners and press releases about virus alerts, definitions of what constitutes a threat and definitions of security are always in process and directly effect what technology is produced.

6 Situated Exclusions and Reinforced Power

Networks are created not just to communicate, but also to gain position, to out-communicate.

(MULGAN 1997, 21)

The term 'digital divide' is shorthand. It refers to the social disparities, diversities, and segmentations within the networked society (Castells 2001; Moss 2002). Limited access to the internet, whether based on incomplete knowledge and 'know-how' or physical infrastructure issues, marginalizes segments of the world's population from the growing predominance of digital communication. On the other side of the divide, those with broad and comprehensive access gain more power and resources, potentially able to direct and profit from their extensive and wide-ranging connections.

Within the antivirus industry, the digital divide is a multidimensional phenomenon. In this chapter I will explore three distinct separations between the information-rich and the information-poor. First, industry professionals confront the seeming universality of internet access. In contrast to their interactions with a 'global village', they must also negotiate the technological realities of national divisions between industrialized and developing societies and the resulting real-world geographic exclusions. Second, white men run the industry. Women are conspicuously absent from the industry. Antivirus industry professionals mirror and reproduce the divisions between men's and women's participation found in many other high-tech industries. And finally, the antivirus industry is grounded in differential access to and the maintenance of secret and exclusive knowledges. The various knowledges that comprise the antivirus industry challenge and reinforce the inequalities and social hierarchies found within larger sociocultural structures. This chapter analyzes the effects of these digital divides on the antivirus industry, as these professionals engage, mobilize, and direct antivirus technological knowledge production.

Geographic Exclusions

Universalisms

Computer viruses do not respect time, space, or place. Computer viruses can span jurisdictions, cross defined boundaries, and spread almost instantaneously. They transgress vocational, temporal, geographical, political, national, and cultural borders. Seemingly rigid segmentations merely dissolve.

> CORPORATE END USER ANTHONY: See, our city has three domains so there are three separate areas of administration. Police and Fire have their own smaller networks and I oversee the largest portion, which is for the rest of the city. And I can keep us up to date. But it is hard to keep the other groups going. And that's how we got hit was that the Police told me that they were up to date and they weren't. It got around them. And since we are the mail servers of the central internet nexus, everything flows through our mail servers. And when it started firing off, it just went around us and it hit Fire and then it came back down and choked us out. We are trying to work on that and getting all the IT groups under one management structure. But government doesn't like to work that way.

Computer viruses dissolve the boundaries and borders between domains such as city administration levels and government departments. Virus outbreaks annihilate divisions and ignore turf wars over demarcated spaces. City government departments, through transnational corporations, are equally vulnerable. The 'internet nexus' breaks down conventional divisions. Whether a city government or corporation or a virus writer, all utilize interconnected networks with various linkages to other networks. They can be physically operating in one country, moving electronically across the world from one network to another, while easily accessing systems on different continents.

This erasure of time, space, and place is intertwined within the antivirus industry. The speed of a malware attack in crossing these boundaries is what fuels the need of and energy driving the industry. Vendors are evaluated on the speed and timeliness of their responses to globalized threats.

> CORPORATE END USER STEVEN: Our vendor, the one that we have a site license with, is for the most part doing a very good job of protecting us before the fact. And when they don't protect us before the fact, they protect us very soon after the fact. A couple of hours. And even when it's something that they do generically, they often, within a couple of hours, will have something that's explicit for us. So, that's fast. I mean, you know, two-hour turnaround!

> CORPORATE END USER KENNETH: Their response time when you e-mail them is just incredible for an international company! I can e-mail them and they will e-mail me within half an hour. That's excellent service! And they have always had really good replies if we have had a problem with something, with the system not installing properly or something, then they come back very, very quickly with responses.

Rapid response time is one of the important evaluative markers of an international vendor's service, and becomes one of the industry's competitive indicators. Thirty minutes to two hours, protecting both before and 'very soon' after the fact, is constructed as 'excellent service'. Corporate end users appraise vendors based on their ability to control response times.

The antivirus industry cannot be understood independently of its instrumental use of time and its management of a chronic sense of urgency. Time for the antivirus industry is in this sense both real and symbolic, continually reproduced and promoted within the industry's everyday practices. For vendors, urgency continually (re)shapes the landscape of common opportunities and normal constraints, illuminating those vendors that have the capability to respond seemingly almost instantaneously. The industry 'lives' with this compression and acceleration of time, reifying it into material processes and identity practices as part of a company's unique networked power and communication.

Virus outbreaks generate a sense of temporal immediacy that also undermines space barriers. With an outbreak, there is instant 'all at once-ness', as the speed of the outbreak creates a total and inclusive field of global contagion.

> RESEARCHER KEITH: Say an AV company in Peru . . . if they see something, it's not only going to be limited to Peru. If there are companies in Peru who have been hit by that virus, by the time the Peruvian company gets a sample, that sample comes from a business that has U.S. and European and probably Spanish e-mail addresses in their address book. So, it has already left the country. And you are never ever going to get ahead of it because it is out of, you know, it has bolted. It's out the stable door. But you can reduce the eventual spread of it because these things always spike fast and die quickly. And what we can do is, we can make them die quicker.

While Peru is identified as 'the local', it is used as a place marker to highlight the speed and global nature of the problem. It is here that a 'mass mailer' infects the local system, moving from the local to the global network, the network in this case defined as the United States, the European Union, and Spain. Focusing on the individualized countries and their relationship within the network, this researcher emphasizes the pace and spread of contagion, and the speed of the potential globalized effect. Alluding to bolting horses, this researcher draws attention to both the accelerated pace of infection and the lack of control over assets displayed by most transnational businesses. The potential for global contagion is used in contradistinction to the job of the antivirus industry to contain the escaping virus. 'What we do' is quickly respond to viruses, preventing local infections from turning into global contagion, which could become a long-term international crisis.

This description of the rapid spread and global threat of computer viruses highlights how spatial and temporal practices are never a neutral part of a discourse (Harvey 1990, 239). Both space and time are symbolic processes, which are fully implicated in engaging, constraining, producing, and maintaining discursive practices (Soja 2000; Munn 1992, 116). Within the antivirus industry, utilizations of time and space are veiled instruments of power, key to making some antivirus companies more practical and commercial successes. While the rapid global spread of a virus necessitates the very existence of the antivirus industry, competing vendors have differing global response times. At the very foundational level, small or new antivirus companies that cannot monitor the world networks twenty-four hours a day, seven days a week, cannot compete when a virus outbreak begins. Having the necessary capital to support transnational offices working around the clock, 24/7 is a major investment, leaving only large, transnational organizations within the industry able to compete against each other. Successful antivirus companies must manage a 'follow the sun' 24-hour clock, always available, always alert, and always scanning the net for spikes, with office locations strategically placed to monitor and service the global network. The sense of global urgency and the necessary corresponding response times maintain the power and privilege of already established large antivirus companies. Managing space and time reproduces the industry's hierarchies and values. Large transnational antivirus companies can then seamlessly be at the 'right place' at the 'right time', keeping order and reproducing industry standards of global response times.

The Antivirus Global Village

The sense of 'place' as residing in a specific nation-state is challenged by the global outbreak of a computer virus. The very technologies that enable multinational corporations to do business more quickly and easily defy the controls and regulations of single nation-states. These transnational technologies also provide opportunities for the development of globally organized criminal networks (Castells 1996). Within the antivirus industry, the implications of these developments are recognized in the articulation of the 'global village'. Malware is seen to have no boundaries here either. Networked technologies dissolve the borders of the nation-state and reinforce the process of de-territorialization.

> RESEARCHER WILLIAM: Well, a virus is a virus. You know, I mean it doesn't really matter where it comes from. I mean, you know, it is a global village now in terms of that. I mean it is remarkable how fast some of these viruses are spread. In the old days, in the very old days, 1988, 1991, 1990, it was Bulgaria which was the top virus writing country. Then it shifted to the Netherlands, up to 1992 when there was suddenly legislation. Then it moved to Russia where the majority of the viruses were coming from so, it's. . . .
>
> I: So it moves around the world?
>
> RESEARCHER WILLIAM: At that time, yes. Right now because of the internet, people can really communicate with each other and it doesn't really matter if Igor is in Moscow and Jack is in New York and . . . well, whatever a Spanish name is, Pedro is in Spain or Mexico or Bolivia. It's because there are no boundaries, they can communicate.

"In the old days" viruses were located in nation-states. They were identifiable by where the virus writer was located. But because virus writers can now communicate their information using the internet and because they also connect across nations, they too now benefit from globalized information exchanges. Through the globalized flow of information and through the increased speed and distribution of viruses, the virus writers' identities and specific locations are obscured.

The threats posed by the virus writers help to unite the global village. Antivirus professionals discuss this global village as an 'imagined community' composed mostly of like-minded netizens (Said 1978). The imagined community of this global village asserts common values and a shared history. It has its narratives, its stories, images, landscapes, historic events, and of course, its threatening villains to help cement the boundaries of proper behavior within the community.

Integral to the sense of community within the global village is the antivirus industry's use of 'Global English'. Everyone I talked with, except one Asian researcher, spoke English. Significantly, this Asian researcher said he would like to join CARO, but would be rejected because of what he labeled as his 'language deficiency'. He would have had to rely on a translator for all his CARO interactions. Since the translators are not actually researchers themselves, and since they are not personally known to the CARO members, the Asian researcher would be rejected. While many CARO members are not native English speakers, all meetings, all internet correspondence, and all 'official' communications are done in English. At antivirus conferences in Europe and Asia, the majority of presentations and social events are conducted in English. A researcher comments on the dominance of English, even at an antivirus conference in Japan:

> RESEARCHER KEITH: One of the reasons [a CARO member] was trying to get other CARO members to go to the AVAR conference [Association of Anti-Virus Asia Researchers] was because they had, the conference organizers, had gone out of their way to make it a friendly conference for English-speaking people. It must have cost them a lot of money to do that because if they were going to do bilingual translation for an Asian conference, I would have thought that Japanese and Chinese would have been the obvious languages to use, but they did Japanese and English. I guess they, therefore, potentially cut themselves off from a potentially large number of potential attendees who speak Chinese in the Asian region. We knew though that a number of the Asian antivirus developers were represented there, some of whom there is very, very limited contact with, still largely because of language issues. But most of them didn't speak English. So we knew they were there with English, they had their own translators. Like the Koreans had their personal assistants and their secretaries and whatever who spoke English and Korean. So they listened to the English translation of the papers and made huge amounts of notes in Korean which they then gave to the Korean antivirus researchers. So those people could have meetings with the English-speaking antivirus developers because they could take their personal assistants, secretaries, whatever, and they could translate for them.

An Asian antivirus conference was bilingual, but not in the dominant languages of the region. English and Japanese were the supported languages. This researcher assumes that all other language groups would bring their own translators. It was also assumed that these translators would speak English. Not speaking English is considered a drawback. Translation issues, however, do not impede viruses. Viruses are able to penetrate language barriers.

> VENDOR TIMOTHY: In a purely technical sense, some virus might stop because they don't happen to work on different [language] platforms. But most of them don't stop. No, if they are carefully done or sufficiently lucky they just go right on through.

If viruses are 'carefully done' or 'lucky', translation into a universal technical language accelerates their global spread. While the lack of understanding of different languages is recognized as hampering both the ease of virus transmission and the smooth communication between industry professionals, the domination of the English language for communication is unquestioned and reproduced as the collective language of the antivirus industry. According to industry practice, Global English is the language of net business, and thus also the language of antivirus security.

The collective myth of an imagined community glosses over or naturalizes the conflicts, struggles, and divisions between social groups (Featherstone 1997). The concept of the technological global village is a gloss that harmonizes its netizens into a single identifiable union. For the antivirus industry, information flows, the use of Global English, and the velocity and global spread of computer viruses nullifies national borders and language barriers.

This antivirus industry's version of the global village is structured through techno-capitalism. Creative technical solutions for computer security are researched, funded, and promoted through corporate profits and investments. The collective myth of the global village naturalizes the conflation of technological progress, internet security, and corporate investments and profits. Consequently, those within the antivirus industry who obstruct or undermine capitalist production and accumulation are critiqued for their lack of commitment to both servicing and protecting the global village's technological structures. Those who do not comply are criticized. An Eastern European vendor 'fails' to adequately market his superior 'golden egg' technological innovation in the global village:

> VENDOR GARY: I see certain parts of the socialistic system, perhaps even some stuff left over from the communist system to a certain extent, but in certain ideologies, certain financial things keeping [aspects of the antivirus community] apart. What is not a good thing, is for someone to rest on the ideologies they have, and therefore because they don't believe in capitalism, they don't believe in marketing. For them to have the 'golden egg' and say, "I have the golden egg and all of the people who work for me have it, and that use our product have it." Okay? So, this minuscule little population over here has that. But because of their ideology, they'll not allow the rest of the world to have it. That to me is a taker. That person will never have, because they don't give. All they have is, "I have this and I want to stand on this stupid fucking principal." Okay? However, the irony of that is that they would typically be the same person that would say, "I can't go with you to take this fabulous vacation in Malaysia because I don't have enough money." There's lots of money out there for everybody. You just have to find a way to be flexible on it and your ideology. And to do what it is you want to do, and get what it is that you want to get out of life, and get the money that you want. And if you're truly happy sitting in a rented flat, you know, in the middle of Eastern Europe someplace. . . .

Geopolitical location, ideological positioning, and technological production are entwined. The Eastern European antivirus vendor should develop, promote, and advance his 'golden egg' and should become a global capitalist in order to contribute to 'saving the world' from malware. By choosing not to promote his product, by limiting the availability of his 'golden egg' to a 'miniscule population', the noncapitalist Eastern European vendor is constructed as naïve and selfish, his ideology and principles dismissed as irrelevant and inflexible, and his geopolitical location in Eastern Europe is collapsed into a political ideology. Eastern Europe is seen as on the periphery of the global village and at the margins of the imagined technological community. Consumer capitalism emerges here virtually unchallenged as the essence of the good life. Consumerism is the vehicle for freedom, empowerment, and happiness. The outdated socialist ideologies left over from communism are negatively compared to consumerism. While antivirus professionals have a duty to provide antivirus software to the world, it is also assumed they are consumers who are choosing, acquiring, using, and enjoying material objects and experiences around the world. Indeed, it is suggested that all antivirus professionals should reap the benefits of their labor. "There's lots of money out there for everybody." Consumption defines the meaning of takers and givers. The 'good life' involves fabulous Malaysian holidays and not living in Eastern European rented flats [apartments]. For this vendor, a person's ability to display and enjoy material commodities reveals a person's ideologies, technological competences, and dedication to protecting the global village.

There was an air of inevitability and acceptance of technocapitalism that pervaded much of the interview discussions. Globalization, capitalism, and technological development were entwined and taken for granted as beneficial and indispensable. It was continually implied that individuals and social systems worldwide should be brought into the techno-capitalist market economy. Another researcher commented about differences among international perceptions of liberties and the homogenization inherent in global business practices:

RESEARCHER MICHAEL: Well, I think when you look at Iraq and France and Germany and the U.S., you're looking at personal liberties. When you look at business, I think everybody's pretty much on the same page.

'Business' collapses historical and cultural distinctions between opposing nation-states. 'Business' puts everybody 'pretty much on the same page', and is the seemingly universal dominant logic and economic rationality pervading their global village. 'Being on the same page' promotes and legitimates the prevailing corporate ideology of globalization within the antivirus industry. The global economic market is in this sense intimately interwoven into the antivirus industry's basic parameters.

Another difficulty within the homogenizing myth of the global village is illuminated by the attempted prosecution of the virus writer. Different sovereignties, jurisdictions, laws, and rules come into play. For example, should claims for prosecuting the virus writer come from the country in which he lives, or where the virus was originally released, or where the resulting damages occurred? Or should claims for prosecution come from all countries where systems were affected? Or should claims for prosecution come from all countries that had victims? Virus writers can also design malware that delays dropping its 'payload', creating difficulties in retracing its technological path and making it almost impossible to reliably establish the originator's identity. What then determines who has the authority to prosecute and punish? Can it be the best evidence rule? Or the first-come, first-served principle? Or do traditional solutions remain in effect?

These unresolved questions limit the action of nation-states to pass laws and inhibit national governments from prosecuting malicious code writers. One state or one nation alone cannot address the threat posed to the globalized network. According to the antivirus industry, the traditional nation-state is a deficient partner in a collaborative effort to battle international cyber crime. Conventional state laws need to be extended beyond one government's too-narrow jurisdiction. The solution within the antivirus industry is to extend the state's functions into a nonterritorial, extra-sovereign space. The international cooperation between various national governments and the antivirus industry after 9/11 is cited as a good example of initial cooperative efforts:

> VENDOR BRIAN: September 11 definitely changed the legal environment because a lot more countries went and ratified and created laws against electronic warfare, against virus writing which is good, which is very good. I want to see more consolidation here as well. I want consistent laws between the countries so that [terrorists and virus writers] don't feel safe in any of the countries. So, I want the virus writing to be outlawed uniformly everywhere.

Because of and since 9/11, some countries amended their traditional statutes on mischief, vandalism, or damage to tangible property. Others created specific provisions against malicious code writers. In the United States, a number of state laws contain more specific sanctions for the insertion or intrusion of a computer virus, and at the federal level, a provision sanctions the reckless causing of damage when a federal computer system is intentionally accessed without authorization. Overall, however, laws, criminal justice systems, and international cooperation have not kept pace with the virus writers' rate of technological change. Only a few countries have adequate laws to address the problem, and of these, not one has resolved all of the legal, enforcement, and prevention problems (United Nations, Office on Drugs and Crime 1999).

Antivirus industry professionals consequently promoted the need to construct a transnational, bureaucratic network of consistent international laws to protect their concept of a global village. Most identified the instantaneous and global form of communication and the consequent need for international laws to prosecute threats to global security, public safety, and consumption. The need for global security generated an international space with an artificial homogeneity among all netizens. Antivirus professionals want consistent transnational laws to protect that imagined space.

After 9/11, the French, United Kingdom, and United States governments all stepped up their security and prosecution efforts against cyber terrorists. As a result, global cooperation between antivirus companies and national governments linked global issues of economic management with policy formations on internet security. The domestic and international became fused spaces through a series of interlinked processes: domestic and foreign economic policy, transnational business and trade, and the passing of consistent international laws and prosecution.

RESEARCHER MICHAEL: On the angle of laws, for instance, the spam laws and the effort towards making global hacking laws and things like that, the EU [European Union] has been stepping up with some of those so it's interesting to see how they're addressing things. We all recognize that

ultimately we need a single law, or something that is relatively the same all throughout the world or it is just going
to be a big mess.

One aspect of this 'big mess' is the specific problem of public international law and the search and seizure of foreign databases via international telecommunication systems. Malware writers increasingly
store their data in computer systems located beyond their own borders
in order to hinder prosecution. In these international investigations of
malware, the direct penetration by prosecuting authorities of foreign
systems generally constitutes an infringement in and of itself. Because
of this type of legal encumbrance, antivirus professionals continually
suggested the need for defense protocols and global laws in order to
protect their homogenized global village and to arrest and prosecute
transnational malware writers, from the millionaire spammers to the
Russian mafia.

I: The internet, does that take away the sense of the global
boundaries?

RESEARCHER WILLIAM: Yes, the only global boundary there is
now is the world. I just read that Zambia was connected to
the internet as the last country in South Africa. So the
world is connected to the internet now. And that means,
you can . . . I mean, right now I am ordering my DVDs in
Australia because of the low Australian dollar. It's cheaper.
So I mean, for me it's the same effort to order from a local
shop, or a U.S. shop or an Australian shop. I just go to one
Web site, buy it, and then it's done. So there are no boundaries any more here.

I: Is that a good thing or a bad thing?

RESEARCHER WILLIAM: Information-wise it's a good, because
you can find all the information you want on the internet.
On the other hand, it is opening the world as well for the
worldwide attacks. Any . . . I can attack any system in the
U.S., the denial of service attack, and it can be to cnn.com
in the U.S., and it can originate from Asian countries, only
because there is no boundary any more.

Distance, time, and space have ceased to be obstacles in commercial transactions. It is as though the logic of the deregulated market has found its perfect instrument in the Web. This antivirus researcher articulates the formation of an all-encompassing political economy—and unitary world civilization—as a commercialized reality. He is the ultimate global consumer. He appreciates the dot-coms of a borderless world for their convenience and prices. Digitalized capitalism reconstructs nation-states into an electronic global consumer village.

As this researcher identifies, however, there is a 'dark side' to this globalized networked access. The entire global village is 'open' and thus at risk of attack from anywhere within the village. The center of United States' corporate news and information is also vulnerable to an assault that can originate from 'Asian countries'. Major transnational corporations are identified and targeted, and are exposed to cyber attacks from seemingly invisible and yet, powerful, enemies. So, while the technology is seen as positively contributing to the removal of boundaries to financial interactions across countries, this unbounded openness also generates risks and vulnerabilities that need to be contained by more technology.

Even though the unbounded global structures of internet communication and financial transactions are praised, there are also articulated tensions toward specific nations. This researcher contrasted the East and West, and the quote by the vendor Gary above focuses on the differences between socialism and capitalism. The borderless nature of this global consumer village is also a problem, as malware is easily accessible and transmitted around the world through potential attacks from anonymous 'others'. National boundaries, which in the past may have hindered the activities of criminals, are seen to have effectively disappeared with the advent of modern telecommunications bypassing traditional border controls.

Recurring Nationalisms

As the quotes above indicate, the antivirus industry is both a product of and promoter for economic, market, and political globalization. The antivirus industry charges itself with policing a world order for 'friction-free capitalism' and with maintaining transnational mobility and network connectivity. Those interconnections, however, exemplify the tensions between globalism and nationalism and provide fertile ground for expressions of national identities. While most of the antivirus professionals quoted above emphasize how a transnational world and global communication flow renders obsolete the old order of national territories and boundaries, they do so by articulating national and regional identities. While highlighting a techno-cultural discourse that promotes and legitimates the prevailing corporate ideology of globalized capitalism, national identities are not transcended. Instead, like the body/computer metaphor, the ambivalences and 'reversible relations' inherent in tensions between nationalism and globalism are exposed.

Within the antivirus industry, nations and regions are more than geopolitical entities. They are also constructions of the character, the culture, and the historical trajectory of a people. Such constructions, by their very nature, include and exclude. The Eastern European vendor is chastised for his lack of a techno-capitalist orientation. 'Asian countries' was used as an example of how a computer virus could attack CNN. Even though computer viral threats are promoted and recognized as global threats, the threats are identified through 'the other' as a nation-state or region. In this sense, the internet does have a geography.

The geography of the antivirus industry within global competition involves a paradox. While researchers cite changes in technology and competition as diminishing many of the traditional roles of location, they also identify specific nations and regions as 'other'. They reveal the double-faced nature of globalization by hollowing out and creating a homogenized identity within the global village. This new imagined space knows itself as unified and distinct from what it excludes as 'outside'. Depending on one's geopolitical position, Africa, China, Eastern Europe, Japan, and the United States can all be differently identified as 'other'. Depending on one's geopolitical location, all these nations are conceptualized as outside the security nexus:

VENDOR JASON: The Japanese market is [pause] despite what some people may believe, particularly the Japanese, it is very undersold at the moment. There are a lot of gaps. There are many companies that are not protected, mainly the smaller companies, but there are many more companies who are protected but not protected adequately.

RESEARCHER MICHAEL: The only difference was that before 9/11 everybody was talking about China. After 9/11, or immediately after 9/11, the concentration went over to Al Qaeda but after recognizing that Al Qaeda didn't pose a threat there, everybody went back to China. They're not sure about China.

I: Is China a threat or is it hype?

RESEARCHER MICHAEL: I think China is a threat in the monetary sense and so you think of, well you could use an attack on the internet to, to gain command and some of that. And it's also a closed society so that people don't know what's going on and therefore you have the conspiracy things and you can always blame things on China.

A joint discussion with an Asian and a Western vendor suggests otherwise:

VENDOR LEE: The problem, where does the problem come from? We can see that there are virus writers. Originally it is from the West—we call it the West including Europe and America, okay? All the non-English speaking, even non-Caucasians we believe is, we call it West.

VENDOR GEORGE: What an extremely odd thing to say. Didn't Stoned [virus released in 1987] originate in New Zealand? Brain [virus released in 1986] originate from Pakistan?

VENDOR LEE: Well, yeah. That is why it is 'original'. Originally it is believed that it is outside. AV coming in to solve problems, if you look at it.

From the Western perspective Japan is seen as 'undersold'. Because the antivirus market is not saturated, the nation is seen to have gaps in its computer security, and consequently, is thought to be naïvely unprotected. China is described as a financial threat, one that will attempt to 'gain command' over the internet. From the Asian perspective, viruses originate in the West, 'outside' their region, such that their local antivirus companies must solve these 'Western problems' in order to protect their own society. Even with the increased speed and pace of communication within globalized networks and even with the world being defined as a single globalized borderless space, antivirus professionals in both the East and West have different visions of this global map. Western antivirus professionals understand themselves as the guardians of universal values on behalf of a world formed in their own image. Eastern antivirus professionals recognize their region as a self-contained and isolated space, one that they must protect from the intrusion of Western technological inadequacies. So, while the intensification of communication flows creates a transnational space, within that space geopolitical identities are actively reasserted by the people interacting there. To talk about global culture is equally to include these forms of cultural contestation (Featherstone 1997).

The contestations over exclusive knowledge groups within the antivirus industry, when translated onto the global stage, are interpreted through the lens of geopolitical identities. An Asian vendor reveals this geopolitical context inherent in the controversy surrounding the exchange of virus samples within the industry:

> VENDOR LEE: About exchanging virus samples, that's a very controversial topic. Historically everyone has been very suspicious of everyone else. They question what they are going to do with them and it built up trust slowly. And I think that also creates a barrier for entry for any new people. And I think some people in Asia have thought of this as almost a policy to keep them out.

The controversy over sharing virus samples within the antivirus industry is interpreted as a trust issue. That trust issue has repercussions on the international scene. Asian antivirus professionals, aware they are not included within the intimate trust circle, interpret their exclusion along geopolitical lines. Barriers to full participation within the industry are decoded through the territorialization of regional states. In response to the global compression and the intensity and speed of transnational information flows, all these antivirus professionals articulate reterritorialized nationalistic imagined communities. All these professionals project onto the 'other' the attenuating fears around submersion and exclusion within a global state.

As a previous quote stated, China is a major technological market, one that Western antivirus vendors both covet and yet approach with reservations. China's internet usage is similar to much of the patterns seen in the West. Its users are young, well-educated, affluent males (Dai 2002). However, the power and control of the Chinese government over the internet and its more nationalized antivirus software industry worries many in the Western antivirus industry. Whereas internet architecture in the West tends to be decentralized and part of the competitive, free-market economy, the Chinese government applies a highly centralized approach to development, based on the strong historic influence of central economic planning and a rejection of political pluralism. The Chinese government attempts to assert effective control over the internet through the introduction of a wide range of pertinent regulations and controls, designed to limit the flow of undesirable information. Western antivirus professionals find it difficult to place their trust in the decisions of these types of governmental structures and officials. Western antivirus professionals thus reject Chinese government regulation of industry standards. They challenge the assumptions supporting the efficacy and security of governmental regulations and the control of computer virus samples.

Thus, historical variations in different countries, according to their history, culture(s), institutions, and their specific relationship to global capitalism and information technology, affect their interpretation of computer viruses and the use of antivirus technology within the global village. Differences in system configurations, infrastructures, bandwidth, interfaces, accessibility, standards, training, business models, and citizen rights and responsibilities guarantee that the antivirus industry in China will be different from that in Iraq or in the United States. Even through antivirus professionals work within systems and networks that are interdependent and global, the industry and its technological applications do not provide the same material and cultural properties in every local space or context of use. Various elements of the interdependent system and their uneven development interact to provide different types and levels of service.

For the antivirus industry, nations are more than geopolitical entities; they are discursive constructs, which by their very nature are symbols of inclusion and exclusion in the 'imagined community' of the global village. The concept of 'inside and outside' the global village is inherently dynamic and open to contestation. Who is inside and who is outside mirrors and amplifies the antivirus professionals' geopolitical location. The industry's perception of the global village is one that is both integrated and fragmented, both united and disorganized, seemingly speaking with one voice while contradicting with another. The global village functions as a uniting explanatory concept for an industry in an increasingly complex, knowledge-based, and dynamic economy. The pressures of globalization challenge and transform the relevant national identities in complex ways, suggesting increasing cultural diversity and hybridization, and also a reassertion of culturally specific identifications.

The identities within the global village are constantly shifting. They are being shaped and reshaped by changing social conditions. Al Qaeda, China, the European Union, India, Japan, Pakistan, and the United States are all potential threats to technological order, depending upon one's geopolitical location. What has been left out of any discussion of globalization and the global village are the nations of the Third World.

> RESEARCHER WILLIAM: I mean everybody is always mentioning the Third World countries. These are also the countries we ship our old systems to, the old operating systems with the known holes, which are easy to infect for hackers because [the holes in security] are documented.
>
> I:. . . but again the fixes are there also, yeah?
>
> RESEARCHER WILLIAM: Yes. But some operating systems cannot be fixed, some holes. . . . Because the machines cannot handle that. All the operating systems will be unuseful. . . . Maybe that's one of the bigger problems that the antivirus industry or security industry should actually give a discount on security products to the Third World countries.
>
> I: That's a nice thought. Could you promote that?
>
> RESEARCHER WILLIAM: I can, but nobody would sell there.
>
> I: Why?
>
> RESEARCHER WILLIAM: You're a commercial company. What I do costs money. Somebody has to pay for that and that's the customer.

This is the world in which networked capitalism functions—the world of global electronic transactions, global information flows, and elite knowledge contestations. As this quote indicates, what is considered 'global' continues to be delineated by very specific market boundaries. The global village contains distinct geopolitical identities, because of and in spite of the global production and distribution of communication technologies. This is a world where producers of technology reproduce socio-structural hierarchies. Instead of globalization and internet connectivity eliminating cultural differences resulting in a unified, homogenized global culture, this quote highlights the brutal consequences of economic and technological rationales that justify maximizing economies of scale and production. The quote explicates the processes by which global communication technologies are actively shaped within capitalist production and consumption contexts; the important political, economic, and social factors that influence organizations to address or ignore diverse technological needs. The quote illustrates how the 'progress' of global transformation is unstable and uneven over the planet, and not easily reduced to generalizing terms such as 'decentering'.

Indeed, on the global scale, the countries most dependent upon networked communication to support and control their technological and financial infrastructures are the United States, Japan, and the member states of the European Union. These are also the countries that have corporations willing to invest in the development of, and to pay for, computer security. A double gap develops where, the less developed networked communication a country has, the more vulnerable it is to this type of threat. Unfortunately, without this technology, it is virtually impossible to compete in the international economic system. Antivirus professionals recognize the growing centrality of internet communication technologies to the structure of international power relations and are concerned about the gap between the information-rich and the information-poor in the digital age. The concern, however, remains abstract, a problem blocked within the industry by markets and commercial necessities and sensibilities.

Antivirus industry professionals draw upon semantic superimpositions of global capitalism and citizenship within their conceptualization of the global village. Through these discourse topics, these professionals draw analogies between infections of biological viruses and threats to the nation-state and global currency flows. Intrusions to computer networks by viruses, denial of service attacks, and spam are constructed through contestations around threats to the global village and advanced capitalism. The computer antivirus industry provides evidence of a transformation into a singular, homogenized transnational socioeconomic and cultural space. However, these professionals also reveal that geography and 'the nation' still matter in a very real sense as local and national geographical specificities continue to shape technological discourses. The social articulation of these differences, however, is a complex, ongoing negotiation.

Social Exclusions

While some antivirus professionals suggest the global village is without borders or boundaries, the double-speak of these professionals suggests a different reality. Their innovations reflect a highly stratified society and reinforce existing socioeconomic disparities. The conclusion of the statement by researcher William above suggests the protection of electronic space is more prevalent and secure in highly industrialized countries than in the less developed world. That type of protection is also going to be more secure for middle-class households in developed countries than for poor households in those same countries (Castells 2003). That type of protection is not available when customers, as end users, cannot access, afford, or update security services. The unprotected become very real casualties amid the material and virtual spoils that go to those with the capital to purchase protection. One's social location within techno-capitalism determines one's level of protection.

Like the geographic boundaries of the internet, social divisions of the internet are also deeply fragmented by the double logic of inclusion and exclusion. The antivirus industry professional is anchored within and draws from the highly educated and technologically advanced groups within the most advanced Western societies. In this sense, the antivirus industry is not separate from the existing social structures, but rather is marked by the same political, economic, and cultural processes. In their discussion of their industry, they reveal how their expressions and cultural meanings are grounded in the same language and symbolic universes of this larger culture.

Indeed, many of the oppressions and inequalities of the larger social structure exist within the industry, established, produced and reproduced as forms of power and social authority. Part of that power and social authority is racialized. Whiteness, Blackness, Asian-ness,

and so on are socially constructed categories with real-world consequences. The inequities inherent in their construction are reproduced
and reinforced within all social, political, and economic institutions.
Importantly, the power and privilege that comes with whiteness is also
reproduced within that inequity.

And the antivirus industry is not an exception. It also draws from
and reproduces these racialized inequities. The majority of CARO
members are white and of European descent. For the most part,
Asians are excluded from CARO and attend only Asian antivirus conferences. As quoted above, Asian conferences attempt to attract
English-speaking Westerners, while Western conferences attempt no
such enticements. Asian antivirus professionals also articulate feelings
of segregation from the power centers of the industry because of the
language barrier. Language conflates with geography and race, ultimately reinforcing white privilege. There are also very few African
Americans within the industry, generally, or who attend the antivirus
conferences. The few that I talked with stated their racial identity was
not a factor within the industry, and yet they also suggested because
they were Black, they generally had to demonstrate their ability above
and beyond their white colleagues. All seem to recognize that the
power centers of the antivirus industry are composed of a white male
majority.

White people, however, often do not see themselves as racialized,
or as privileged as a result of their racial identity (Giroux 1997; Kendall
2001). Their whiteness (their racial category) is seemingly invisible to
them, their power taken for granted and naturalized as inevitably
based on education, or upbringing, work ethic, and so on. They are unable to recognize their privileged social location as systemic and supported by historical and cultural processes. Indeed, many whites assert
they are 'color blind'. However, race is significant to the way we all see
ourselves and the way others experience us. It is, "perhaps, second
only to gender in terms of salient identities used in interpersonal relat-
ing" (Hill and Thomas 2000, 194). Gender, race, ethnicity, and class
cannot be denied as important social issues within the antivirus industry as it reflects and negotiates with larger social structures. The rest of
this section will focus on gender as one of those variables and explore
its visibility/invisibility.

The Gendered Culture of Technology

Like whiteness, gender is a visible/invisible part of the antivirus industry's conceptualization of itself, taken for granted in the industry's everyday interactions. Like whiteness, the industry professionals' gendered relations are not isolated from the larger social structural tensions in the culture of the internet, which are connected to more widespread patterns of social inequality. Indeed, the antivirus industry's gendered relations express, in a contradictory and conflictive pattern, the interests and values embedded in cyberspace itself.

In general, cyber cultures have been shaped as masculine (Haraway 1999; Wyatt et al. 2000; Whelan 2001). To say that control over technology is a core element of masculinity is not to imply that there is one masculinity or one technology. Different forms of masculinity are more prevalent in relation to different areas of technology. Masculinity, like femininity, takes historically and culturally specific forms. Within cyberspace, women and men have new opportunities to launch businesses and political initiatives, and to share with others across the world. Within highly digitalized industries and infrastructures, women and men encounter new opportunities, new experiences, and new roles. However, this does not mean that they can fully escape older forms of power and inequality. The confines of existing hierarchies of economic power still ground many of their interactions. Women must still fight for greater equality in opportunities and rewards with men. In this regard, it is naïve to overestimate the emancipatory power of cyberspace in terms of its capacity to neutralize gender distinctions.

Out of the thirty-three people agreeing to talk about the industry, only six women were interviewed: Three were vendors, three were corporate end users. All identifying characteristics have been removed so these women remain anonymous.

The lack of women antivirus professionals is apparent and recognized by most within the industry. In 2001, CARO elected one woman into its membership. A year before her selection, a CARO researcher discussed the diversity of members in CARO.

RESEARCHER KEITH: I don't know, more than two-thirds of the current members of CARO anyway don't have English as their native language. There are Hungarians, Bulgarians, Russians, Germans, Poles, I can't think, Norwegians, Dutch yeah, it's a. . . .

I: No Japanese, nobody from Asia?

RESEARCHER KEITH: There are no Asian members of CARO, there are no South American members of CARO, there are no [pause] yeah, there are no African members of CARO. I was going to say. . . .

I: And are women in CARO?

RESEARCHER KEITH: There are no women in CARO.

This researcher attempts to identify the diversity of CARO membership as based on native languages. He begins listing the various nationalities that comprise CARO. Until he is prompted and interrupted, other regions of the world and women remain invisible in this diversity list. His sense of diversity is based on northern European origins. CARO consists basically of white Western males. The diversity of languages and European national origins veils the exclusion of gender and race, and other geographical regions. One of the recognized power blocks of the industry is unnoticeably and invisibly uniform.

In contrast to this male researcher, women experience the antivirus industry as masculine. One woman corporate end user stated in 2004:

CORPORATE END USER ALEX: This is a male-orientated industry.

I: So why do you think there are so few women in the industry?

CORPORATE END USER ALEX: Well, why is there only one woman in CARO? I don't even think she is in there still, is she? Well, work from there and work back. I started writing an article on women in the industry and I interviewed [names four women] and I was told that it was of no interest whatsoever, and I was never going to publish it. I don't think there is no. . . . A lot of people don't want to come into an industry that doesn't want them, I mean it is as simple as that. And, you know men tend to be more technical. I mean there are a few people, there are a few girls in soft-

ware who are very, very technical. Very clever girls. But
there is like two to every fifteen men.

It is assumed that the majority of men are more technical than
women. It is also implied that the 'girls' who do come into the industry
are of a higher standard, they are 'very, very technical' and 'very
clever'. One African American confirmed this observation when asked
about women in the antivirus industry:

> Sometimes it seems like mainly they have a lot more to
> prove so they are a little bit more business-like, Okay? And
> a lot less, I have never seen any eccentric women in the AV
> industry. It's like they always, you know. I can identify with
> it, being Black. So, you always have to be better than the
> next guy. So I understand where they are coming from. So,
> it is easier to relate.

Women's specialist ability is seen as outstanding and superior to
the ordinary antivirus industry professional. The self-identified Black
man 'relates' to women's experience of needing to be 'better than the
next guy' in order to compensate for the assumptions accompanying
their minority statuses. However, the woman quoted above suggests
that there is no interest in these exceptional women specialists. This
corporate end user states she was told she would never publish an article on women antivirus professionals. While she disagrees, she identifies the industry's lack of interest or care in knowing about these few
women, these very technical, 'very clever girls' within the industry.

She also states that people do not join an industry that 'doesn't
want them'. Feminist scholars have continually documented practices
of exclusion that effectively discourage women from participating in
many scientific disciplines. Interview questions did not address ex-
plicit forms of discrimination, such as differentials in pay and employment status. Both men and women interviewees, however, articulated
the more subtle forms of dissuasion identified in feminist research—
such as failure of scientific communities to acknowledge important
work by women experts, chilly climates, prescribed gender roles, the
masculine cultures of science and technology, and female underrepre-
sentation. All these dissuasions are documented as affecting women's

interest in pursuing scientific and technical careers (Wyatt et al. 2000).

Indeed, the corporate end user above suggests that the lack of interest in these exceptional women contributes to the lack of women within the antivirus industry. She also suggests that the industry does not create a welcoming environment for these women. Replicating other high-tech industries, many of the professionals within the antivirus industry acknowledge the subtle and sometimes not so subtle barriers that effectively work to keep women from entering and being a part of the industry.

Historical Absence of Women in Technology

One explanation suggested that the absence of women is grounded within the general infrastructure of IT.

I: Let's talk about women in the industry.

VENDOR JASON: There aren't that many actually.

I: Yes, I noticed. Any explanation for why?

VENDOR JASON: I think the IT industry as a whole, a lot of people, particularly on the research and development side, and by research I mean software research and virus research, it tends to be viewed as a very male thing. And a lot of the people who are doing it are the sort of people who have had a computer at home since they were teenagers and played computer games at home. Not all of them by any means, but there is a lot of that. So I think that women tend to do that less. I think they've got more sense [laughs]. But, there are women in the industry. There are some very talented women programmers and virus researchers, but they are very much in the minority.

Cultural notions about gender are used as a resource to explain the difference in development of technological interest and knowledge. Here women are a minority within the antivirus industry because as teenagers, they 'sensibly' chose not to play and master computer games, while men actively cultivated these technological proclivities. Playing computer games as a teenager is seen as reproducing masculine cultures and hierarchies of power, eliminating women later on from the digitally-driven circuits of technological communication and information. The development of a realm of expertise in those teenage years engenders an authoritative and techno-strategic direction to male development.

In this sense, women's exclusion from the antivirus industry is seen as merely layered upon the long-standing male domination of information technology. The games, skills, and language of white, bourgeois, heterosexual teenage masculinity are seen as structuring the way antivirus technology, as an industry, claims knowledge, space, and vocational place. The antivirus industry is seen as simply extending these already established patterns of segregation. It is not that women are incompatible with technology; it is that men are more compatible. Cultural attitudes and dispositions as forms of cultural capital facilitate and nurture the development of this gendered digital divide. In a tautological formulaic discourse, women are not equally present in the industry because they have been excluded in the past. Two vendors talking together address the invisibility of women in technological fields after their university education:

I: Why do you think there are so many less women in the AV industry?

VENDOR BRIAN: Well, in general, in the technical fields there seems to be less women. I mean I studied physics, there was like. . . .

VENDOR JEFFERY: Two girls per hundred [laughs].

VENDOR BRIAN: . . . yeah, about that. . . .

VENDOR JEFFERY: Same for us. . . .

VENDOR BRIAN: With my other products, with development systems, when I go to conferences, we can see the same thing. Five percent women. It's just a general thing. I mean, there have been studies and whatever involved to find why this is the case.

VENDOR RONALD: Why are there less women in this industry? Whoa. I have never even thought about that. Pure speculation. When computers first came out they were a guy thing, they were for like the nerds and the geeks and you know, that's just the way it was. You didn't find very many women who were computer literate or really passionate about them. Or if you did it was only like one in every thousand. I can't explain it any other way, I don't know.

These statements of social and historical differentiations result in an oversimplified binary opposition between the women as nontechnological and invisible and men as historically technologically competent, conspicuous, and employable. Because of their historical absence, women are absent in the present. The historical segmentation in the technical fields is reproduced in today's industries, revealing the complex relationships between knowledge, power, and technology. Mastery of technology in the past bestows power on these men in relation to women who are seen as lacking this expertise. From this perspective, the antivirus industry's gendered relations are historically determined by larger social structural conditions. However, the issue of women's visibility and participation within the industry is more complex than these prevalent but simplistic historically determined oppositions.

Biological References

The other factor used by antivirus professionals to explain the lack of women in the industry was biological reproduction. Industry professionals cited the female reproductive cycles as preventing women from fully dedicating themselves to the demands of virus outbreaks. It is assumed that women's family responsibilities inhibit their investments in the industry, and thus render women less productive. The inference is that rewards go to the more committed antivirus professionals who choose to invest in and focus on their careers.

> RESEARCHER CHARLES: I think the type of security work that we all do, surely you will agree with me on this one, it requires very long hours and availability, many hours when you might like to switch off and have a big break. That is much more difficult for women to do, particularly if they have a family.

I: Let's talk about women, women in the industry.

RESEARCHER WILLIAM: [laughs] I know one.

I: Why do you think that is?

RESEARCHER WILLIAM: I don't know. It's a hard business because it is quite a demanding business, sometimes 24/7
when there are big threats. No matter how you turn it, if
there are kids in the family, the wife gave birth to them. So,
of course there are some parts of getting the kids grown up
of course that are also part of the male, the men. But no
question, in the beginning, it's definitely the girl. Preg-
nancy and well, two or three children later, they start
again. They have to catch up those years. In this industry,
that's a killer because it is moving so fast.

The initial biological differences between male and female are
elaborated into very different long-term career trajectories. Women
with families are different from men with families. The 'killer' pace
of transformations within the antivirus industry excludes the child-
rearing, nurturing, domestic female. Childless women or single-
parent fathers are invisible within this explanatory formula. Instead,
explanations of women's lack of participation within the industry an-
chor gender identities in nostalgia and traditional family values.
Women do not work in the antivirus industry because they cannot
dedicate themselves to the demands of 24/7 availability. Women do
not work in the industry because they cannot perform within its time
commitment framework. Their dedication and focus is distracted by
other responsibilities. Work within this twenty-first century elite technological industry is described by utilizing the culturally dominant
masculinity discourse supporting a nineteenth-century industrialized
workforce.

This language of patriarchal euphemisms functions as a legitimation for both the present state of gendered relations and what it means
to be an antivirus professional. Industry professionals assume a body
of knowledge, skills, and work ethic that are used as the explanatory
framework for the lack of women within the industry.

Sexualized Imagery

Besides the role of non-computer-game-playing, child-rearing mothers, antivirus professionals pinpoint another identity for women: women as sexual objects of virus writers. All types of malware have used representations of female sexuality. In explaining the social engineering inherent in some e-mail subject lines and Web sites, a researcher describes how sexually misleading topics lure the naïve user.

> RESEARCHER KEITH: It is completely understandable as a matter of human psychology that people will click on that. If it is called "Anna Kournikova's Tits," people are going to double-click on it because there are a substantial proportion of people in this world who use computers who want to see pictures of Anna Kournikova without her top on.
> I: I think that that would be mostly male?
> RESEARCHER KEITH: But, in a corporate site, I mean even in today's world, that still, you know there is just proportionately more of those people, right?

To this researcher, it is completely understandable that Anna Kournikova's breasts seduce 'people in this world who use computers' to double-click and accidentally download a viral payload. The conceptualization of the social engineering behind the malware writer is logical and rational. Women and women's body parts are objects to be voyeuristically gazed upon. It is understood that women's bodies allure men against their better judgment, titillating them to do things they ordinarily would not do. Women as computer users and women as part of the corporate sites are invisible and not considered.

Women's representation as seducers can also be used against malware writers. A researcher uses a 'sock puppet' analogy to acquire secret information from malicious code writers:

> RESEARCHER CHARLES: Also, quite often women are very good at lulling the person into a false sense of security and getting information out of them that they wouldn't always give. Which, if you are investigating something, is worthwhile. In fact I. . . . Because we often have sock puppets,

you know that concept? I have one with a female name, for exactly those reasons. I get more responses from somebody. It is quite fun sometimes.

This researcher enjoys the seemingly disembodied aspects of the internet that allow him to play the role of a woman, lulling malware writers into revealing their secrets. Recognizing and utilizing culturally mandated understandings of women, he manipulates the unaware malware writer. Besides the ability to lure and manipulate, women were also mentioned as secretaries and clerks, and the 'nice voice' of the head of the help desk.

CORPORATE END USER EARL: And certainly the organization that I currently work with, the only woman I can think of in that, is the head of the help desk function, which, you know, nice voice, that sort of thing I guess. I mean, it's very sexist I guess.

These antivirus professionals demonstrate how women are disempowered and marginalized in everyday language. Women are invisible unless they are in some way sexualized. They have the power to seduce and lull. They are body parts. They are segmented into help desks for their nice voices or recognized as clerks or, as one corporate end user stated, the 'house-wifey types' in the secretary pool.

The professionals within the antivirus industry identify historical conditioning as inhibiting women's decisions to join the industry, perceive family commitments as prohibiting women's fulltime commitment, and recognize and reproduce the larger social–cultural frameworks that see women as sexualized objects. This sequence of understandings gives life to the rationales explaining why women are invisible within the antivirus industry. What this discourse achieves, however, is the justification of a whole series of exclusions based on the dichotomy between masculine and feminine. This generates a chain of analogous oppositions that align men with employability, commitment, and dedication, and women with seduction, passivity, and the body.

Gender is not just about difference, but also about power. Maintaining women's difference in these ways replays the binary dualisms coupling women to nature and the body, and men to technological expertise and competence. Technical competence generates power and is seen as central to the dominant cultural ideal of masculinity. Women, on the other hand, are seen as disinterested in technology. Their absence, except as sexualized body parts and in nurturing roles, accommodates and reinforces ideals of stereotyped femininity.

It should be stated that this coupling does not originate in particular individuals or just the antivirus industry, but is reflexive of a broader cultural context. The constructions of masculinities and femininities are complex processes. There is not one monolithic masculinity or one femininity, and not all men are competent with technology. However, within the antivirus industry, demonstration of mastery of this technology bestows power. The more mastery is displayed, the higher the person is raised in status and respect in relation to others who lack this expertise. And usually, the higher the status and respect, the more material rewards this skill brings. Critiques of masculinities are left unspoken or alternative masculinities are invisible, silenced by a hegemonic masculinity that stifles their expressions. For example, a corporate end user describes the arrogance in the contestations over marketing and service priorities. Her metaphor of the struggle is expressed through sexualized animal dominance rituals:

> CORPORATE END USER ANDY: Obviously the worst ones are the PR ones, the marketing ones, the big management and the financial guys. But I think a lot of it is a show, you know, locking horns in public. Yeah, like a couple of stags you know.

Masculinity is articulated through fatherhood, technological competence, and stags locking horns. Alternative interpretations, alternative explanations, and alternative metaphors for gendered struggles remain unspoken. The antivirus industry operates within a traditional hegemonic masculinity, silencing the numerous other perspectives of being men and women.

Successful Women in the Antivirus Industry

Most antivirus professionals are aware that gender relationships are a contested domain in much of the world. Many identified the few successful women within the industry as examples of a lack of specific industry bias and discrimination. Two vendors discuss the gendered relations within their own companies:

> VENDOR BRIAN: My chief technical officer was a woman. She has actually become a CEO of another company. And my, one of my managers, she looks after all the development centers around the world. She is a woman. There are at least five or six or seven other women I know in very senior executive positions.
>
> VENDOR JEFFERY: Well, in HR. . . .
>
> VENDOR BRIAN: Well, HR is traditionally . . . but definitely not only in HR. Like you have people in quality control, you have people in development, you have people in tech writing, you have people in translation, you have people in computer development.
>
> I: And this is unusual then?
>
> VENDOR BRIAN: I used to work for [Company Name] before. We had two female secretaries and they were like, looked up to. Like that is what you can achieve if you are a woman, okay? However, the rest of them, they were males and like for better or worse, I don't know. Then I came to [Company Name], it was just, wow!

There are a wide variety of workplace cultures and practices within the antivirus industry. One need not presume that there is a single uniform behavior pattern in all companies to argue that the antivirus industry in general reflects the culture of dominant gendered relations. Indeed, these professionals identify the success of five or seven women in one company. These antivirus professionals highlight these women's success as senior executives and linked them with technical competence. Their success is suggested to have been attained on seemingly gender-neutral, universal, and standardized evaluative markers. The surprise articulated, however, also reveals how gendered marginalization continues.

The characteristics of hegemonic masculinity are projected onto the behavior of women whose success as antivirus professionals is analyzed in terms of their ability to behave in similar ways to men.

Women's success is measured by comparison to the technical attributes of men, achieved by climbing the corporate ladder, ignoring family, and other distractions. Women learn to react as men, to negate traditional feminine behaviors, and are rewarded accordingly. A woman corporate end user comments:

> CORPORATE END USER CHRIS: Well, women can be emotional. You know, it's interesting you know when—I had to go to a board meeting recently and give a presentation. And someone was dialing in and it was really interesting because he kept challenging me and challenging me. But you know I handled it really well, to the point that people in the room were starting to roll their eyes at this guy. And I think that's it. Women just have to, because women can be much more emotional. You have to have that disconnect. You can't take these things personally. And if you can manage that, you are going to succeed. These people aren't attacking you, you know. Some of them are just making themselves look bad, but they're not attacking you. If they're challenging your position or your decision, it's not you per se.

This corporate end user suggests there is a women's way of knowing, a kind of essentialist women's way of responding to the world. She suggests women are more emotional and to be successful, they need to 'disconnect' from these emotions. Women need to learn that attacks that seem personal are merely impersonal challenges to decisions and positions. Women need to transform themselves into the hegemonic masculine ideal, and be more objective, rational, and detached. Indeed, acknowledging the antivirus industry is shaped as masculine, she suggests women need to manage themselves, adapting to these criteria in order to succeed. Even as the industry gives women new opportunities to launch themselves and assume traditionally masculine roles, it does not mean that these successful women can fully escape older forms of power and inequality. The antivirus professional is expected to model her transformation on an image of technical competence, individualism, and nonsensuality.

She must voluntarily come to see her seemingly 'feminine' sensibilities as both at odds with and inconsequential to the realities of the industry.

Women constructing themselves 'as if they are men' generate individuals in the image of the dominant model of the rational, cool, objective, scientific Northern European/North American male. The sense of being this kind of man is seen as a neutral value, as merely part of successfully 'doing business'. A male vendor describes his business philosophy:

> VENDOR MARK: It may sound as a cliché, but as far as my employees are concerned, I couldn't care if they are black, white, pink, male, female, or whatever. As long as they can do their job, they are valuable members of the team. There are lots of clichés about women being better managers, women being worse managers, women doing this, women doing that. I don't really see that, especially in the technical level. You either can do it, or you can't do it. It really doesn't matter what you are and what color you are.

This vendor, in attempting to be fair and neutral, describes a kind of objective universal body unmarked by gender, race, physical disability, or culture. He erases the specific contexts provided by embodiment. His erasure is premised on the sense that he can be a neutral observer, outside and above, able to evaluate work efficiency and yet decree neutrality. His is the 'modest witness', the legitimate and authorized ventriloquist for the objective world, seemingly adding nothing from his mere opinions (Haraway 1997, 23). His language is sanitized, abstract, and yet full of euphemisms of embodied markers that he simultaneously denies. He is seemingly removed from the harsh reality he is talking about; his gender, his race, his social location are invisible. He is focused exclusively on the output, 'as long as they can do their job'. He decrees blindness to issues of inequality and points to his version of political neutrality. By ignoring the historical, social, and political contexts of embodiment, he naturalizes the marginalization of Blacks and women by cementing and legitimating end results. He requires 'blacks, whites, pinks, males, and females' to model themselves on an image of those who traditionally have been considered successful. This is a structural pattern with significant cultural consequences, giving priority to the everyday white masculinity of corporate business practices.

The material body of men and women remains a constant factor within the antivirus industry. Bodies have certain undeniable material qualities that are culturally determined and discursively managed. Bodies are tied to both their physiology and to the cultural contexts within which they operate. Feminist scholars argue that 'realism', dominated by elite, white, male practitioners, is a patriarchal discourse that renders women invisible. Women are invisible in the politics of the antivirus industry, seen only as 'domesticated' figures necessary to family life and nurturing members, part of the help desk or the secretary pool, or sexualized to lure the unsuspecting male. Projections of women's 'feminine' sensibilities lull and entrap unwary male virus writers and their victims. However, these feminine sensibilities and ways of being in the world must be eliminated in office politics. In the cacophony of electronic networks that threaten to overwhelm the body and render it obsolete, men's and women's experiences within the antivirus industry demonstrate how gendered sensibilities reproduce inequalities, contestations, and hierarchies inscribed within the larger structures of technological capitalism.

Knowledge Exclusions

However much antivirus industry professionals can be conceptualized as 'information-rich', they all still struggle within their own industry over the resources, stakes, and access to information flows. Status hierarchies within the antivirus industry, whether an IT corporate administrator or a top-level antivirus researcher, are based on the manipulation of and access to information. The establishment of boundaries between the industry's own 'information-rich' and 'information-poor' re-entrench forms of social authority and contribute to the proliferation of social inequalities.

Antivirus Knowledges

Distinctions between malware writers and antivirus professionals are continually grounded in each group's technological sophistication and knowledge sets. Both are experts by definition as each has mastered structural and operational aspects of current technology and computer code. However, according to antivirus professionals, the similarities stop there.

Unsurprisingly, all antivirus professionals consider the knowledge grounding their industry's software to be superior to the knowledge of any malware writer. Antivirus software designs are based on complex and distinct yet integrated knowledge sets from a variety of highly specialized scientific professionals. The antivirus product is not merely the 'virus detection engine' developed by researchers to counter malware effects. The knowledge supporting the antivirus product is the combination of researcher and developer. Besides the researcher's expertise, antivirus knowledge is also the technological details that support the rollout of the full antivirus product within an entire corporation.

This contribution to the antivirus product is seen by some as increasingly vital to the development of antivirus software, over and above the seemingly overrated contribution of the researcher. Some see the most significant knowledge set within the industry as the ability to consistently and simultaneously roll out antivirus software across multiple transnational platforms, without negatively affecting the corporates' day-to-day functions.

> VENDOR MARK: Antivirus researchers, almost by nature have the view of their world as one machine, because they work on the one machine. It takes a somewhat different frame of mind to design a product which is deployable on tens of thousands of machines in large environments. Virus researchers certainly aren't the best people to either design that, or to make decisions how the thing is best deployed. They do have, of course their function when it comes to fighting viruses and analyzing viruses. But just to give an idea, in a typical antivirus product, the virus engine, the thing which discovers viruses, is maybe one twentieth, five percent of the code which makes up the whole of antivirus. The rest is built by professionals who haven't seen a virus in their life, and, but we have on the other hand seen what corporate problems are, what corporate ways of deploying the

product is, and how the average corporate has to function in order to live.

In this view, antivirus researchers are too narrow, focusing their knowledge accumulation on one machine, one virus. According to this vendor, these researchers are necessary, but their knowledge contributes only five percent to the antivirus product. The other ninety-five percent of the product is not virus related. Ninety-five percent of antivirus software code is grounded in other fields of knowledge entirely and is instead focused on efficient and effective deployment and use within the corporate environment. The professional knowledge required to 'deploy' antivirus software within the business climate is unrelated to the researchers' specialist knowledge about viruses. This knowledge set is from 'professionals who haven't seen a virus in their life'.

As articulated here, not all knowledges are equal. Both researchers and the specialists who roll out antivirus software produce powerfully persuasive accounts about what is significant and necessary. Each is influenced by social practices and commitments. The antivirus industry is, in this sense, embedded within and reflects various contentious symbolic orders and disputed power relations. Each specialized knowledge is subject to challenges and rankings from others.

Ultimately, the relatively weighted specialists' knowledges combine to produce the antivirus product. Researchers' expertise and developers' knowledge of corporate usage and deployment processes merge, with each vendor competing to increase response times. Creative innovations must be continually generated, as both the technology and malware writers transform the field, and as competition between worldwide vendors increases within the techno-capitalist economy. Innovations in the antivirus product, however, also come from another knowledge system. In describing the components of antivirus software, this same vendor describes the end result as a combination of knowledges from scientific methods and the creativity of artists thinking 'outside the box':

VENDOR MARK: It is an art. It's—almost by definition, it's something scientific because they're using computers and they're using well-defined scientific methods. But you have. . . .

It's also an art because you have to have a good nose to vary
your procedures or to vary your techniques, as in if and
when new challenges are put in front of you. So it's not
something prescribed, "Thou shalt do it this way." We are
constantly trying to do things better, faster. And that requires a bit of improvisation. And improvisation, of course,
pushes science into art. Art is usually art because, to use a
horrible expression, they think out of the box. They try
new things, mostly of course, irrelevant things. But sooner
or later, they stumble upon something which is useful.

Antivirus software development is seen as linking art and science,
improvisation with controlled, systematic methods. It is significant,
however, that the 'scientific method' is highlighted as the preferred
knowledge structure. The artistic contribution occasionally 'stumbles
upon something which is useful'. The use of 'well-defined scientific
methods' and formal design procedures are important to prove that the
program will consistently do exactly what it says it will, and so avoid the
gap in the corporate environment between software expectations and
actual performance. The artist's stumbling methods, however, are also
used to highlight the ways in which product developers need to be creative and innovative, responsive not only to mathematical proofs but
also to the requirements of, and implementations within, the real
world. Combining creativity and inventiveness, the development of antivirus software is not bound by traditional scientific knowledge structures. It must constantly and continually generate new solutions as the
technology changes and malware writers conceive new strategies. Developers of antivirus software must 'think out of the box'.

Virus Writer Knowledge

It is this alternative 'outside the box' requirement in the development
of antivirus software that generates questions about the feasibility of
hiring malware writers into the antivirus industry. Mastery of technology is part of the malware writer's skill set (Taylor 1999, 15). The unethical, criminal, and destructive aspects of malware writing, however,
are unacceptable to the antivirus industry. The contrasts between
those obtaining knowledge about the security of systems by illicit,

unauthorized means, and those in charge of protecting those systems, do not generate stable working relationships (Taylor 1999, 101). Besides stigmatizing the malware writers' actions as ethically deficient, the antivirus industry also charges them with lacking comparative technical knowledge. Even though they are recognized as technologically more savvy than the average end user and even though they have demonstrated a flair for manipulating code, of 'thinking outside the box', they are unsuitable technologically to be part of the antivirus industry.

> RESEARCHER THOMAS: Ethical principles aside, we do have, most antivirus companies, virtually all of them have a very, very strong policy. We never ever hire a known virus writer. Especially these days, especially with most of the modern viruses. To create one you have to know much less, I mean like in comparison much less, than to be able to find and remove it. So we have to know how to find the virus. We have to know the internals of each and every like, Microsoft Office file format, how to look inside. What does the virus look like? Where does it compile inside its application? How you find it? How you remove it? So, the knowledge of a virus writer is useless to us. The Windows virus is on the rise now and the guys who write them, they know much more than the average guy who writes something like Melissa or LoveLetter. But, as I said, the most talented virus writer doesn't make a good antivirus researcher.

Antivirus vendors all have specific policies for not hiring a known virus writer. However, the subject still surfaces as industry professionals are continually questioned about virus writers' related technical knowledges and skill sets. For antivirus professionals, questions about hiring a virus writer become contestations about knowledge competencies. Antivirus professionals continually articulate and promote antivirus knowledge as legitimate and superior, and worthy of economic investment. Virus writers are excluded not only as unethical and untrustworthy, but also as lacking sophisticated knowledge and technical skills. They are negated as unqualified to legitimately participate in securing the information network. Indeed, from this researcher's position, breaking into a computer system does not demonstrate any competency or skills. It merely illustrates the problems of that software program. Demonstrating the inadequacies of computer systems does not provide original computer security information or new information about software engineering, scientific testing methods, or the art of cryptography and encryption. From the researcher's perspective, a direct comparison between the 'good antivirus researcher' and the virus writer merely illustrates the superior knowledge of the researcher. While this seems an obvious statement, it reveals how all knowledge sets are context-dependent. Knowledge systems are full of tensions and negotiations as 'knowers'' assertions and practices rank and exclude others from cultural or economic resources (Foucault 1972). Hiring a virus writer to work within the antivirus industry interferes with the industry's boundary maintenance, which must continually demarcate the seemingly obvious differences between each of their knowledges and technological competencies.

Knowledge in this sense is not detached and independent but is integral to the operations of power within the antivirus industry. The industry's formation and accumulation of knowledge, including its grounding in science, art, and corporate sites are not disinterested or unbiased. Antivirus knowledge systems are in this sense not a neutral science, but delineate an analytic space that is specialist, exclusive, and proprietary. These knowledge systems provide the basis for excluding the stigmatized virus writer. These knowledge systems are also the basis for the industry's rationale as security providers for the networked corporate infrastructures. These exclusive and specialist knowledge systems are the grounding of the antivirus industry's power.

Cyber Terrorists

The threat of cyber terrorism to the global infrastructure is downplayed by most within the antivirus industry. Besides viewing cyber terrorism as a media ploy, cyber terrorists' knowledge systems are also negated as technologically innocuous. The antivirus industry does not accept terrorist organizations as technologically sophisticated enemies capable of crippling technological infrastructures.

RESEARCHER DANIEL: What kind of effect do you expect? Can you imagine the terrorists of Bin Laden sitting around in their cave and discussing what nasty trick to play on the world? Okay, let's disable their internet gaming. Come on!

This researcher critiques terrorists merely playing a 'nasty trick' by disabling internet gaming. He trivializes both Bid Laden's cave dwelling, and the effect of destroying the recreational aspects of the internet.

Another critique is that if terrorists' actions are supposed to induce fear, crippling the internet would be merely a costly annoyance. For cyber terrorism to be effective, it would need to be used in conjunction with other hostile acts to cause 'terror'.

RESEARCHER DANIEL: Even if such a virus was distributed involving serious effects on all the sites, it is still not going to kill anyone. It is not going to take down the stock market or whatever. But nevertheless, it is going to cause billions [of dollars] of damage to all those people who won't be able to trade. Again, the emphasis is on the damage. But this kind of thing is not suitable for terrorists except maybe as one additional thing to do along with the main attack. I do think that all those talks about cyber attacks and so on are a little bit overplayed. But it is not necessarily a bad thing because I think that the reason why they are overplayed is in order to get funding and that means getting money for security measures. But it is a good thing to have such measures in place. So, even though I don't quite approve of the means, the goal might be a good one.

Cyber terrorism is considered merely one element within a terrorist attack, one whose likelihood is strategically overplayed. The representation of terrorists as 'cave dwellers attacking globalized computer gaming' is used to illustrate the lack of real-world, life-and-death danger from cyber terrorism. Cyber terrorists are excluded as cave dwellers and outside the high-tech security world. In other words, they are absent from the information network.

However, damage caused by attacks on globalized stock market trading is also highlighted to illustrate the financial impact of potential attacks. 'Causing billions of damage' is significant. This kind of double-speak surrounding cyber terrorism highlights again the superiority and necessity of the antivirus industry's knowledge systems. This researcher simultaneously denigrates the technological competency of cyber terrorists, while also illustrating the need for financial backing to implement computer security. The antivirus industry and its knowledge systems are integral to protecting the stock markets' technological architecture and information systems. However, cave-dwelling terrorists are negated as non-serious threats to those systems. So, while negatively assessing the technological capabilities and impacts of cyber terrorism, this researcher also pinpoints how the malicious manipulation of digital information could have far-reaching effects on the nature of economic, social, and political development in an information-based society.

CARO: Denouncing the Knowledge Elites

Antivirus knowledge is bounded with economic structures, influencing what is appropriate knowledge and what is profitable to know. The economy drives much of the antivirus industry's research and development. In general, research and development does not exist 'out there' external to economic incentives. Rather, research and development is an ongoing social accomplishment, constituted and reconstituted through major financial backing, which demands profitable results and applications. As such, 'knowing' cannot be understood as an 'objective' fact. Because 'knowing' is enacted in response to economic criteria, its status is always provisional and responsive to economic priorities.

'In the beginning', CARO researchers, as part of the research and development of the antivirus industry, formed a knowledge monopoly. CARO researchers were accepted as an independent source of knowledge. As an altruistic community support for the industry, CARO researchers were seen as a counterbalance to industry marketing and profit motives. Increasingly, however, CARO is reinterpreted as an instrument of corporate profit and unaccountable power. With the contestations of 'alternative' knowledge groups, such as REVS, AVIEN, and AVIEWS, CARO's authority over the conduct of the antivirus industry has diminished. For some, CARO is no longer useful and now merely perpetuates a power relationship that serves its members economic agenda more than industry priorities.

VENDOR TIMOTHY: They did it that way back when it was a cottage industry because they wanted to know, they wanted to trust things. Before they sent viruses to something, they wanted to trust it. And they decided it was easier to trust a person than a company. And they're quite right. It's easier to trust a person than a company. However, the problems with that, well they're self-evident. There's obviously, what happens if you, the accident occurs and you can't decrypt? What happens is, it's an awful incredible amount of power in the hands of the CARO members, because they suddenly become immensely marketable because the companies want these viruses.

Evolving from a cottage industry where everyone knows who to trust and what the hierarchies are, the industry has become a multi-tiered, multibillion-dollar, high-tech enterprise with competing logics and rationales. Respect for CARO was based upon its unique knowledge and its operation above economic dictates. As such, it had influence over the workings of the industry and amassed both knowledge and power accordingly. This vendor suggests, however, that while the entire antivirus industry has changed, CARO members continue to profit from their exclusivity. This quote implies that many in the industry recognize CARO members accumulating information as personal capital, generating and exercising profit and power exclusively for themselves. They are 'immensely marketable'.

Another negation of the CARO knowledge system focuses on the actual membership of CARO. Over time, the CARO researchers moved up the corporate ladder, assuming non-researcher-oriented positions as managers and directors, training others 'below' them to analyze malware, and 'handing off' the secret and dangerous viruses to others. CARO as an organization becomes simply a sample-sharing apparatus, with the members earning large salaries for merely giving virus samples to others to analyze.

VENDOR TIMOTHY: They've either gone on to do something else or they've progressed sufficiently far up the chain that they don't spend all their day analyzing viruses anymore.

They have employees to do that. They are managers. They are directors. So what they must do is get the viruses from CARO and use their trust network inside that company to give them to somebody who will look at them. So, what CARO then becomes is this kind of a meta-trust thing where you don't trust that person X will do the right thing with the viruses directly, but you trust that person X will give them to someone that he knows will do the right thing with them.

CARO is a 'meta-trust' organization, dispersing information through its members' establishment of a trust network. 'Knowing' about computer viruses is not a static embedded capability or stable disposition of antivirus professionals, but rather is constituted and re-constituted as these professionals form more trust networks that now include specialized others known to 'do the right thing'. CARO becomes a knowledge-based organization that reifies information. Through their monopoly over information, its members manage information and disperse it to form other exclusionary relationships. And again, CARO members profit from that process.

Whatever one's position within the antivirus industry, most agree that 'doing business' within the industry has changed. Authority and power shift over time with the transformations of technology. The nego-tiation for dominance and influence within the industry is a continual battle. Through that process, the standing of the CARO members as the elite in technological knowledge is exposed to public critique. The ex-clusive fraternity based on mutual trust that labors for the betterment of the networked global community is reassessed as a mired 'old boys club'. CARO has become an easy target in a globalized world where it is seen as an organization of only a few white, male, elite scientists who are 'im-mensely marketable' and thus profit from their enforced exclusivity.

Power is fluid. It acts through individuals. CARO's elite status is denaturalized and questioned, and its status is illuminated as contin-gent and transitory. The 'big personalities' are seen as an old guard from a different time. As the industry personnel change over time and as the status of those in power positions changes, the industry is recon-figured to accommodate new voices.

End Users' Knowledge

While the CARO member's status is challenged as 'the' elite within the industry, most antivirus professionals still recognize a more general digital divide between the technologically competent and incompetent. The boundary between the two levels, of course, is porous and changing, depending upon the relevant technology used. Generally though, most end users are seen as unable to fully participate in, much less control, the technology that constructs global networked communications. Given the highly complex nature of modern antivirus software, end users are seen as too unaware and uninformed to be entrusted with technological responsibilities. In fact, end users continue to demonstrate to the industry their inferior technological understandings in their daily misuse of antivirus products.

> VENDOR TIMOTHY: The way that all these products work, in the past, the history of behavior blockers is, as soon as the monitor notices something suspicious, it will pop up a box, and it will ask the user, "Program XYZ is about to write to your master boot sector. Should this action be allowed, yes or no?" And this was great. But unfortunately it passed the buck entirely on to the customer. The user then had to decide whether Program XYZ should be allowed to write to the boot sector. Silly. The user didn't understand the question. The box said, "Program XYZ is trying to write to your master boot sector." But what the user understood, through no fault of their own, was "Mumbledy mumbledy mumbledy mumbledy mumbledy, yes or no." "Mumbledy mumbledy mumbledy mumbledy yes, no," is going to get a "yes" answer.

This vendor creates a narrative about Program XYZ and an abstract user. The 'behavior blockers' he discusses are computer programs that monitor the 'behavior' of other programs. Behavior blockers allow end users to intercept and prevent unwanted programs from performing or continuing their processes. As part of an antivirus software package, the behavior blocker component allows its abstract users a choice. It is assumed that users should easily understand this choice and correctly choose which processes should run. However, the users in this narrative, 'through no fault of their own', do not understand the question or context of the question. The users are seen as hearing and seeing 'mumbledy mumbledy mumbledy' and choosing incorrectly. The contrasts between the assumptions and expectations of the developer of this computer program and the users' assumptions and expectations suggests a significant breakdown and division in technological understanding.

When the program asks for directions, the end users are expected to be 'information-rich' and thus understand both technological conditions and the context of the questions asked. All users are expected to have knowledge about these technological rules and resources. Designers in this sense are expecting some replication of their expert knowledge structures within their end users. Indeed, designers often take for granted their own contexts, their own knowledge systems, and their rules and resources, silently building these into the software. Significantly, while the vendor's quote above implies he is aware and can articulate the end user's perceptions as 'mumbledy, mumbledy, mumbledy', the perspective of the designers' narrative assumptions remain invisible.

The designers' expectations are, however, omnipresent and pervasive, and structured within the very context of the choice, 'yes' or 'no'. In this sense, both designers and end users apply narrative assumptions in their interactions with the questions being asked. Human action is a central aspect of both of their technological interfaces, in the actions associated with embedding structures within a technology during its development, and the actions associated with appropriating those structures during the use of the program (Pollock 2005).

Only the end user, however, is portrayed as naïve and uninformed and as misinterpreting taken-for-granted assumptions. Only the end user is depicted as lacking knowledge and misinterpreting choices into garbled gibberish. Instead, the computer program can be seen as embodying misinformed assumptions about its end users (Latour 1999). During its development, the designers instilled their erroneous assumptions about end users into the software.

Depicting this designer's expectations as naïve, garbled, confused, and as lacking knowledge about the end user significantly reverses this power/knowledge nexus. Instead of the program portrayed as rational, accurate, and merely instrumentally requesting directions, reversing the power/knowledge assumption suggests that the designer needs educating, and the program's design is in error. The designer can also be seen as ignorant about necessary and significant information. The programmer has designed a security weakness into the program by assuming end user knowledge, and has programmed those assumptions into the software. Instead of portraying the real user as answering incorrectly and ultimately infecting his computer with a boot sector virus, the computer program can be seen as asking an invalid question and thwarting support of end users in their technological labors. The narrative of the end user as not understanding and as knowledge-poor reveals assumptions built into the software.

Current technological innovations are taking into account this type of divergence between antivirus designers and their end users. New antivirus technology largely eliminates end user choice options by automating the process in the background. Because users have continually responded 'yes' to the question they assume is being asked of them, antivirus designers attempt to remove those questions completely. Basically, most antivirus professionals reject educating end users. The majority of antivirus professionals interviewed do not believe that training and educating corporate users about the assumptions, rules, and resources inherent in antivirus software is a viable answer. Instead, antivirus professionals, including corporate IT managers, want to take this type of responsibility out of the end users' 'ignorant' hands.

CORPORATE END USER EARL: Education doesn't work because unfortunately we have people who are human. It's a fact of life. We all make mistakes. We all forget at some time, which is why one of the things that we influence the antivirus towards was the on-access type of systems. Because if you give the user a choice of doing something right and doing it wrong, one would like to think that there is a fifty-fifty chance with no education at all. But even with education, it seems to me they're doing it wrong a hundred percent of the time. Humans should be taken out of the decision process wherever possible, because they'll get it wrong. So where you can automate it, you should do so.

Corporate end users want automation. They are attempting to 'influence' the industry toward taking humans 'out of the decision process'. In comparison to the faultless, flawless, idealized machine, humans are imperfect. Humans 'get it wrong one hundred percent of the time', and thus need to be removed from the technological equation. As one researcher stated, "Everything made by software can be avoided by software." Again, technology is portrayed as this neutral entity, objective and removed from error-ridden end users.

Automation will make antivirus software invisible to the end user by locating it in hubs, ISPs, ASPs, and on every server and cell phone. Being invisible, automation is an attempt to control the divergence between designers' and end users' knowledge sets. Automation does not allow the user the option to choose to do other than what the designers have dictated. Automation is the industry's effort to manage the technology in response to end users as (bad) choice-making agents. In this sense, end users have not been passive or simply shaped by antivirus technologies, but they are also shapers of that technology (Pollock 2005). Vendors must make adjustments to their software in order to protect the net. Automation becomes a means by which antivirus companies attempt to maintain control and profits by securing technology against 'misinterpretation' by both designers and end users. Modifying the software to accommodate the real world by making it invisible and by adapting it to both designers' and end users' 'limited' knowledge, reveals the changing and indeterminate nature of antivirus software as a technological artifact. This indeterminate and adaptive nature of antivirus software interweaves and links both designers and end users (Pollock 2005).

It is significant, however, that many of these antivirus professionals will not run automated antivirus software on their own machines. With their expert knowledge and insight into both technology and the economic structures that support technological development, they do not trust the technology that is enmeshed within a larger corporate mindset.

CORPORATE END USER ANTHONY: Personally, I don't want anybody on my computer except me. I don't want anything happening on my computer except me. I am very diligent when it comes to my software package and wanting to access the internet for updates. And I picked the most restrictive options to where I know when it wants to go out, it tells me what it's got for me before it installs it. I don't let it do anything automatically.

I: Why are you the only one that you want on your computer?

CORPORATE END USER ANTHONY: I don't trust them. You know, I mean, I might trust Jo's software company if they were small and they have some idea as to the fact that they were being idealistic to some extent. But I don't trust Microsoft. You know, they burned us often enough on a variety of different issues. I want to know what is going on before it's doing it. I don't trust them to do it in the background without my knowing about it. I think that I'm somebody who is in the know and am going to be a lot more concerned about it than the average person. The average person, they don't want to know about computers. They want the computer to work like an automobile, you know. You get in, you turn it on, and it drives. You don't know anything about what is under the hood. You don't know anything about how everything works. You just want it to work right and you just want it to work.

Acknowledging antivirus software as a corporate enterprise, this antivirus professional rejects automated protection and security. He does not trust the corporate structures behind Microsoft's Windows Update. Indeed, he rejects allowing a company like Microsoft to work 'in the background without my knowing about it', which highlights how automation implies scripts of trust, dependency, and a kind of technological intimacy. This corporate end user believes his own knowledge competencies are more than adequate to counter malware efforts.

Most antivirus professionals do not see the rise of the 'knowledge society' translating into a technologically informed citizenry. The 'average person' just wants the technology to work and to work 'right'. Function is depicted as the users' highest value as the 'average person' lives in blissful ignorance. 'Looking under the hood' is negated. The 'average person' voluntarily cedes control and understanding of technology to the technological experts.

However, the 'knowledge society' creates a hierarchy of technical expertise whose employability is grounded in that informational digital divide and on the dependency of end users as these 'average people'. The maintenance of boundaries between the 'average person' and the antivirus elite is based on security and the need to protect networked communications. End users do not have enough knowledge, cannot be educated in proper security techniques, and are not seen as having the desire to learn. The digital knowledge divide disproportionately benefits the technological elite, maintaining their 'information-rich' status and the corresponding financial dominance in the world of e-commerce and computer security.

What emerges from this hierarchical and exclusive power arrangement around security and secret knowledges is the formulaic reproduction of these exclusive and hierarchical relationships throughout the industry. At all levels within the antivirus industry, the professionals come to mirror these trajectories of power. The lowly corporate end users, the 'Bobs and Janes from accounts', become 'information-rich' within their own organizations. Responding to the exclusivity of CARO and REVS, they established their own exclusive and privatized knowledge sets through AVIEN. So, while the criteria of a technological elite is relative to its positions within the industry, all antivirus professionals throughout the industry appropriate privatized knowledge and construct themselves within similarly-ordered exclusive communities. And they all seem to elevate themselves above the rest of the netizens they deem to protect. It is a continual chain of hierarchical segregations and socioeconomic fragmentations that, together, structure the everyday relations within the industry.

For example, a corporate end user articulated what he thought was the foundation for his own employment security:

CORPORATE END USER ANTHONY: One of the prime sources of job security is to know all the stuff and be careful who you teach it to.

This corporate end user establishes his authority and expertise through knowledge and information that remains obscured and unintelligible to the uninitiated. His privatized knowledge simultaneously creates a hierarchy of technical expertise while denigrating the uninitiated as lacking and as not knowing enough. The corporate end user joins in the new concentrations of information 'wealth' as part of the global technological elites, the 'informational bourgeoisie' who dominate the arenas of information society, reproducing the patterns of inequality based on reduced access to information (Castells 2001). The power to exclude from the loops of information and communication flows is realized as the uninitiated are sidelined and the techno-elite self-promote with their privatized knowledge. Thus, many of these antivirus professionals become technocratic–financial–managerial elites, occupying the leading positions within their organizations.

Elites, no matter their relative ranking, need to remain clearly distinct from the 'average person'. Their knowledge needs to be sacrosanct. Industry professionals negotiate daily over the ranking of their knowledges and their corresponding exclusive relationships. It is a political and practical struggle for power. At risk are both the ability to protect the net, and the exclusive and seemingly private knowledges that generate power and authority. The power and authority created from successfully protecting the net helps in securing successive acquisitions of trusted secret knowledge. Power and knowledge infuse each other.

The relations of domination within the antivirus industry networks are critical to understanding how this industry functions. It is characterized by constant contestations among groups as they limit the escape of secret and exclusionary information. Based on a seemingly unique beneficent community service orientation that seeks to keep global technological infrastructures safe and secure, the industry is also interwoven with economic considerations. The capitalistic enterprise at times runs counter to the beneficent community service ethos. The logic guiding the acquisition and maintenance of privatized knowledge becomes an expression of domination as it reproduces hierarchical inequalities. The antivirus industry is in a continual struggle over the meanings of security and threat, and the industry's relationships to protected and private information.

An antivirus product is therefore not just a technology. It is a technological tool and organizational form that protects information, generates knowledge, and distributes networking capacity. The distribution results in the segmentation and concentration of power into the hands of assorted technological elites. The various power hierarchies share secret information among their own members, but block it from others through security rationales, excluding and inhibiting individuals and groups who are not integrated into their networks. The antivirus industry is a social space of conflict and competition, where professionals struggle to establish control over technology and information that are constantly threatened and constantly transforming. The antivirus industry produces a product designed to protect a global communication network. The antivirus product is the result of evolving human actions enmeshed within information capitalism.

Works Cited

"AVIEN—Anti-Virus Information Exchange Network." http://www.avien.org/ avien.html (accessed September 10, 2006).

Baudrillard, Jean. 1975. *The Mirror of Production*. Translated by M. Poster. St. Louis, MO: Telos Press.

Beck, Ulrich. 1999. *World Risk Society*. Oxford; Malden, MA: Polity Press.

"Big Bucks." 2006. *Virus Bulletin*. http://www.virusbtn.com/news/virus_news/ 2006/07_01.xml (accessed September 10, 2006).

Bigo, Didier. 2002. Security and immigration: Toward a critique of the governmentality of unease. *Alternatives: Global, Local, Political* 27 (1): 63–92.

Bijker, Wiebe. 1995. *Of Bicycles, Bakelites, and Bulbs: Towards a Theory of Sociotechnical Change*. Cambridge, MA: MIT Press.

Bloom, Leslie Rebecca. 1996. Stories of one's own: Nonunitary subjectivity in narrative representation. *Qualitative Inquiry* 2 (2):176–197.

Bourdieu, Pierre. 1985. Social space and the genisi of 'classes'. *Theory and Society* 14:723–744.

Burke, Anthony. 2002. Aporias of security. *Alternatives: Global, Local, Political* 27 (1):1–27.

Burke, Brian E., and Rose Ryan. 2005. *Worldwide Secure Content Management 2005–2009 Forecast Update and 2004 Vendor Shares: Spyware, Spam, and Malicious Code Continue to Wreak Havoc*. http://www.idc.com/ getdoc.jsp?containerId=34023 (accessed November 20, 2005).

Button, Graham, and Wes Sharrock. 1998. The organizational accountability of technological work. *Social Studies of Science* 28 (1):73–102.

CARO. http://www.caro.org (accessed September 10, 2006).

Casey, Catherine. 1995. *Work, Self and Identity after Industrialization*. New York: Routledge.

Castells, Manuel. 1996. *The Networked Society*. Oxford: Blackwell Publishing.

————. 2001. *The Internet Galaxy*. Oxford: Oxford University Press.

————. 2003. Informationalism, networks, and the network society: A theoretical blueprint. In *The Network Society: A Cross-Cultural Perspective*. Northhampton, MA: Edward Elgar Publishing.

Cheney, George. 1998. 'It's the economy, stupid!' A rhetorical-communicative perspective on today's market. *Australian Journal of Communication* 25 (3):25–44.

Ciborra, Claudio. 2002. *The Labyrinths of Information: Challenging the Wisdom of Science*. Oxford: Oxford University Press.

"Cyberspace Invaders." 2002. *Consumer Reports* 67 (6):16–20.

Dai, Xiudian. 2002. The internet in China: Towards a digital economy with Chinese characteristics? *New Media & Society* 4 (2):141–162.

Delio, Michelle. 2004. "Cashing in on Virus Infections." *Wired News*. http://wired-vig.wired.com/news/infostructure/0,1377,62558,00.html (accessed June 7, 2006).

Derrida, Jacques. 1997. *Politics of Friendship*. Translated by G. Collins. New York: Verso.

"The Doomsday Click." 2001. *The New Yorker*, May 28, p. 100.

Douglas, Mary. 1992. *Risk and Blame: Essays in Cultural Theory*. New York: Routledge.

Easterby-Smith, Mark, Richard Thorpe, and Andy Lowe. 1991. *Management Research: An Introduction*. London: Sage Publications.

Ericson, Richard, and Kevin Haggerty. 1997. *Policing the Risk Society*. Oxford: Clarendon Press.

Featherstone, Mike. 1997. *Undoing Culture: Globalization, Postmodernism and Identity*. London: Sage Publications.

Fine, Michele. 1994. Working the hyphens: Inventing self and other in qualitative research. In *Handbook of Qualitative Research*, edited by N. K. Denzin and Y. S. Lincoln. Thousand Oaks, CA: Sage Publications.

"Flaw in Microsoft Word Used in Computer Attack." 2006. *New York Times*. http://www.nytimes.com/2006/05/20/technology/20zero.html (accessed September 10, 2006).

Foucault, Michel. 1972. *The Archaeology of Knowledge*. New York: Tavistock Publications.

Giroux, Henry. 1997. *Pedagogy and the Politics of Hope: Theory, Culture and Schooling*. Boulder, CO: Bergin and Garvey.

Gordon, Sarah. 1994. "The Generic Virus Writer." Paper read at International Virus Bulletin Conference, at Jersey, Channel Islands. Available from http://www.research.ibm.com/antivirus/SciPapers/Gordon/GenericVirusWriter.html (accessed October 14, 2007).

Hall, Stuart. 1991. Ethnicity, identity and difference. *Radical America* 3:9–22.

Haraway, Donna. 1997. *Modest_Witness@Second_Millenium*. New York: Routledge.

———. 1999. A Cyborg manifesto. In *The Cultural Studies Reader*, edited by S. During. London: Routledge.

Harrison, Jane, Lesley MacGibbon, and Missy Morton. 2001. Regimes of trustworthiness in qualitative research: The rigors of reciprocity. *Qualitative Inquiry* 7 (3):323–345.

Harvey, David. 1990. *The Condition of Postmodernity: An Enquiry into the Origins of Cultural Change*. Oxford: Blackwell.

Helmreich, Stefan. 2000. Flexible infections: Computer viruses, human bodies, nation-states, evolutionary captialism. *Science, Technology & Human Values* 25 (4):472–491.

Hill, Miriam, and Volker Thomas. 2000. Strategies for racial identity development: Narratives of Black and White women in interracial partner relationships. *Family Relations* 49 (2):193–201.

Himanen, Pekka. 2001. *The Hacker Ethic: A Radical Approach to the Philosophy of Business*. New York: Random House.

Huysmans, Jef. 2002. Defining social constructivism in security studies: The normative dilemma of writing security. *Alternatives: Global, Local, Political* 27 (1):41–62.

ICSA. http://www.icsalabs.com/ (accessed September 10, 2006).

Johnson, Mark. 1987. *The Body in the Mind*. Chicago: University of Chicago Press.

Jordan, Tim, and Paul Taylor. 1998. A sociology of hackers. *Sociological Review* 46 (4):757–780.

Kendall, Francis. 2001. *Understanding White Privilege*. http://www.uwm.edu/~gjay/Whiteness/Underst_White_Priv.pdf (accessed October 14, 2007).

Klein, Hans K., and Daniel Lee Kleinman. 2002. The social construction of technology: Structural issues. *Science, Technology & Human Values* 27 (1):28–52.

Krause, Keith, and Michael C. Williams. 1997. Preface. In *Critical Security Studies: Concepts and Cases*, edited by K. Krause and M. C. Williams. Minneapolis: University of Minnesota Press.

Krebs, Brian. 2005. "A Billion-Dollar Boondoggle?" *Washington Post*. http://blog.washingtonpost.com/securityfix/2005/08/a_billiondollar_boondoggle.html (accessed September 10, 2006).

———. 2006. "Bringing Botnets out of the Shadows: Online Volunteers Monitor Illegal Computer Networks." *Washington Post*. http://www.washingtonpost.com/wp-dyn/content/article/2006/03/21/AR2006032100279.html (accessed September 10, 2006).

Lakeoff, George, and Mark Johnson. 1980. *Metaphors We Live By*. Chicago: University of Chicago Press.

Lather, Patti. 2004. This is your father's paradigm: Government intrusion and the case of qualitative research in education. *Qualitative Inquiry* 10 (1):15–34.

Latour, Bruno. 1988. *The Pasturization of France*. Cambridge, MA: Harvard University Press.

———. 1999. *Pandora's Box: Essays on the Reality of Science Studies*. Cambridge, MA: Harvard University Press.

Lessig, Lawrence. 1999. *Code and Other Laws of Cyberspace*. New York: Basic Books.

Levi-Strauss, Claude. 1987. *Introduction to the Work of Marcell Mauss*. Translated by F. Baker. London: Routledge & Kegan Paul.

Loader, Ian. 1999. Consumer culture and the commodification of policing and security. *Sociology* 33 (2):373–392.

"Love Bug Virus Creates Worldwide Chaos." 2000. *The Guardian*, May 5, p. 1.

Lupton, Deborah. 1994. Panic computing: The viral metaphor and computer technology. *Cultural Studies* 8 (3):556–568.

MacKenzie, Donald, and Judy Wajcman. 1985. *The Social Shaping of Technology*. Buckingham: Open University Press.

Martin, Emily. 1994. *Flexibile Bodies: Tracking Immunity in American Culture from the Days of Polio to the Age of AIDS*. Boston: Beacon Press.

Mauss, Marcel. 1967 [1925]. *The Gift*. Translated by I. Cunnison. New York: Norton.

Melossi, Dario. 1994. Normal crimes, élites and social control. In *The Futures of Criminology*, edited by D. Nelken, London: Sage Publications.

Moss, Jeremy. 2002. Power and the digital divide. *Ethics and Information Technology* 4 (2):159–165.

Mulgan, Geoff. 1997. *Connexity: How to Live in a Connected World*. London: Chatto & Windus.

Munn, Nancy. 1992. The cultural anthropology of time: A critical essay. *Annual Review of Anthropology* 21:93–123.

"New Computer Virus Circles Globe." 2003. *Wall Street Journal*, May 13, p. D3.

Orlikowski, Wanda J. 2000. Using technology and constituting structures: A practice lens for studying technology in organizations. *Organization Science* 11 (4):404–428.

Orlikowski, Wanda J., and Stephen R. Barley. 2001. Technology and institutions: What can research on information technology and research on organizations learn from each other? *MIS Quarterly* 25 (2):145–165.

Orlikowski, Wanda J., and Suzanne C. Lacono. 2001. Research commentary: Desperately seeking the "IT" in IT research—a call to theorizing the IT artifact. *Information Systems Research* 12 (2):121–134.

Parikka, Jussi. 2005. *The Universal Virus Machine: Bits, Parasites and the Media Ecology of Network Culture*. Available from http://www.ctheory.net/articles.aspx?-id=500 (accessed February 3, 2007).

Pollock, Neil. 2005. When is a work-around? Conflict and negotiation in computer systems development. *Science, Technology & Human Values* 30 (4): 496–514.

Poster, Mark, ed. 2001. *Jean Baudrillard: Selected Writings*. 2nd ed. Cambridge: Polity Press.

Postman, Neil. 1993. *Technopoly: The Surrender of Culture to Technology*. New York: Vintage Books.

Rosenberger, Rob. 2004. "Sophos Now Urges 8,760 Antivirus Updates per Year, per Computer!" *VMyths*. http://www.vmyths.com/column/1/2004/5/2/ (accessed June 7, 2006).

Ross, Andrew. 1995. Science backlash on technoskeptics. *The Nation* 261 (10):346–350.

Said, Edward. 1978. *Orientalism*. London: Routledge & Kegan Paul.

Sassen, Saskia. 2002. Towards a sociology of information technology. *Current Sociology* 50 (3):365–388.

Sobchack, Vivian. 1998. Beating the meat/surviving the text, or how to get out of this century alive. In *The Visible Woman: Imaging Technologies, Gender and Science*, edited by P. A. Treichler. New York: New York University Press.

Soja, Edward. 2000. *Postmetropolis: Critical Studies of Cities and Regions*. Malden, MA: Blackwell Publishers.

Suchman, Lucy. 1994. Working relations of technology production and use. *Computer Supported Cooperative Work (CSCW)* 2:21–39.

Taylor, Paul. 1999. *Hackers: Crime and the Digital Sublime*. London: Routledge.

Thomas, Douglas, and Brian Loader. 2000. *Cybercrime: Law Enforcement, Security, and Surveillance in the Information Age*. London: Routledge.

United Nations, Office on Drugs and Crime. 1999. *United Nations Manual on the Prevention and Control of Computer-Related Crime*. http://www.uncjin.org/Documents/EighthCongress.html (accessed September 10, 2006).

"Virtually Unprotected: An Insecure Nation." 2005. *New York Times* (Late Edition [East Coast]), June 2, p. A24.

Wall, David, ed. 2001. *Crime and the Internet*. London: Routledge.

Wark, McKensie. 2004. *The Hacker Manifesto*. Cambridge, MA: Harvard University Press.

Weiner, Annette B. 1983 [1976]. *Women of Value, Men of Renown: New Perspectives in Trobriand Exchange*. Austin: University of Texas Press.

Weldes, Jutta. 1999. Introduction: Constructing insecurity. In *Cultures of Insecurity: States, Communities, and the Production of Danger*, edited by J. Weldes, M. Laffey, H. Gusterson, and R. Duvall. Minneapolis: University of Minnesota Press.

Whelan, Emma. 2001. Politics by other means: Feminism and mainstream science studies. *Canadian Journal of Sociology* 26 (4):535–581.

"Worm Brings Down PCs and Networks." 2004. *New York Times* (Late Edition [East Coast]), May 4, p. C10.

Wyatt, Sally, Flis Henwood, Nod Miller, and Peter Senker, eds. 2000. *Technology and In/Equality*. New York: Routledge.

Index